Accounts Payable - My Life Past Due

David Arthur Walters

Published by David Arthur Walters, 2024.

ACCOUNTS PAYABLE - MY LIFE PAST DUE

First edition. November 21, 2024.

ISBN: 979-8230238898

Written by David Arthur Walters.

The Black Virgin Visits Brooklyn

THE CONTROVERSIAL "SENSATION" EXHIBIT that opened at the Brooklyn Museum of Art on October 2, 1999, certainly received sensational responses from the public, such as the filing of law suits, the hurling of dung, public vomiting, and attempted iconoclasm. The epicenter of the cultural upheaval was The Holy Virgin Mary painted by Chris Ofili, a young British artist of Nigerian descent. The image portrays a black woman decorated with some shellacked elephant dung the artist claims is symbolic of his African heritage. An odd assortment of female buttocks clipped from pornographic magazines seems to flit about her head like butterflies.

"Sensation" attracted a curious crowd to the museum. However, based on what was seen and heard in the media, most people would not have given a farthing to see the show. Nonetheless, the symbolic elements of the controversy are invaluable and could, if taken advantage of, work a transformation of dung into gold or of foolishness into the wisdom it presently occludes.

For instance, if the subject of The Holy Virgin Mary is the esoteric Black Virgin who presides over the Underground Stream flowing in its spiral course throughout the Hidden Church, then her apparition, perhaps unwittingly made manifest by Mr. Ofili, presages events of biblical proportion.

According to occult tradition, the Black Virgin's appearance precedes a carnival of feminine equality and liberation. A poor compassionate woman shall commune there with mankind, and from the virginal black earth shall emerge a son who shall reveal the Secret

Doctrine in the chasm of his poetic ambiguities: those who seek the Grail in the gap shall behold the face of Mother Night on the threshold of bliss.

The Black Virgin prophecy appertains to the long-awaited liberation of man's feminine side from the violent patriarchal oppression of his forefathers, and to the ensuing procession of the Matriarchal Age of Love. Some thinkers now believe that women are almost liberated. However, they expect a male backlash rather than a love fest to follow. They opine postmodern man has been so badly whipped by modern feminism that he has lost his sublime sense of ultimate male utility; that is, his identification with some higher purpose than becoming, for example, an Internet or Wall Street whiz, movie star, or sports idol. Hence he is expected to strike out violently in a last-ditch effort to erect his self-dignity.

Nonetheless, we find nothing new in postmodern man's misogyny, psychological weakness, and reliance on brute force to redeem himself: it would be a classic mistake to blame his typical behavior on the current Women's Movement.

Fortunately, however, for all those concerned, women are experts in the struggle for personal identity, wherefore they have much to contribute to the male struggle, just as the long struggle of slaves for their freedom helps to emancipate all men. Yes, indeed, perhaps feminist expertise may be the key to the mysterious evolution of sexual peace. Wherefore, when the prophecy is fulfilled, man shall come to equal terms and merge with the real woman fully exposed: the War Between the Sexes shall end in bliss.

In the interim, until the peace treaty is signed, the Black Virgin, the gap between the father and the son, must be whitewashed. A week before Christmas, Mr. Heiner, a 72-year old retired teacher, feigned sickness, slipped behind the Plexiglas barrier and smeared white paint on The Holy Virgin Mary because he and his wife believed the image was "blasphemous." A museum spokesperson called his act "incomprehensible." The vandal was charged with felony criminal mischief. The painting was promptly cleaned and re-displayed. But elsewhere the whitewash has had centuries to dry: the ideal mother resides immaculate (unspotted) in her candle-lit niche, a glowing ornament to emasculated virtue, yet a real source of confusion to men still in their senses. Her retinue of ideal ladies-in-waiting are legion, one and sometimes more for each man. She is the lost mother each man seeks in his wife, she is the first housekeeper or *oekonomikus,* she is the principle of propriety on a pedestal, she is the trustee of native identity, she is prime productive private property. And she is much more than all that: she bears a burden beyond man's comprehension, laboring where he is incompetent to the task.

But let us return to the Brooklyn Museum case of dung in hand. On the one hand, a protester demonstrating against "Sensation" hurled dung at the museum. Some time after Mr. Heiner smeared white paint on the detested image inside, another man outside doused the museum with red paint for unknown reasons. On the other hand, 200 New Yorkers who assembled in Washington Square Park paid a dollar each to don a latex glove and hurl dung at a portrait of Mayor Rudolph Giuliani depicted as a madonna. Reporters revealed that the police raided the apartment of one Stephen Powers, a graffiti artist who disclosed on a radio talk show that he was responsible for staging the protest. A great deal of material was seized, including an antique set of brass knuckles hanging on his wall: Mr. Powers was arrested and charged with the criminal possession of a weapon. Joey Skaggs, the man who actually designed the mayor's portrait, was barely mentioned in the reports.

The dishonored mayor, characterized by his liberal foes as an anal-retentive conservative, wanted to halt the museum's funding, cut off its utilities, and evict it from the public facilities. He denounced the exhibit as "sick". He was eventually overruled by Judge Nina Gershon, who held that the mayor and the city were threatening the neutrality required of government in the sphere of religion.

So far none of this is very astonishing in a city where horses are forced by the city government to wear diapers and where pooper-scoopers are a common appliance. Nor is it surprising that the 'Sensation' exhibit included, much to the horror of animal rights activists, dismembered animals in large containers of formaldehyde.

Now then, as we can see in the symbolic context, Mr. Ofili's intentions were irrelevant when he created the image The Holy Virgin Mary we have so conveniently appropriated for our various excursive interpretations. If he had malice in his heart, his heart will surely suffer. Nevertheless, a few pious folks in Brooklyn are probably burning candles, making mysterious signs in thin air, kneeling and saying special prayers before a facsimile of his work-perhaps a photo clipped from the catalog or the newspaper. Shall we charge them with bad taste, or with idolatry?

Some sympathetic souls believe a little superstitious ignorance might be healthy for vulgar people despite our own noble aesthetic and religious convictions. In any event, no matter what our perspectives and prejudices might be, we should thank Mr. Ofili and his ilk for playing their roles, that we may play ours.

We should also thank New York City Mayor Rudolph Giuliani for his intolerance and his vigorous litigious opposition to "Sensation" The mayor plays the part of a character many generous liberals love to hate: that of an orderly, parsimonious and obstinate mayor sitting on the throne of Babylon under which he is occasionally self-moved to deposit in a box his various execrations in the form of regulatory commandments. Liberals rarely receive mercy under his tarnished seat of power which doubles as a ceiling to all below. Liberals can only hope his angels will fly him and his portable throne elsewhere. Be that as it may, wherever his seat of power may move him, his inhospitality towards the Black Virgin during her visit to Brooklyn has only served to further illustrate the enormous power she holds, even over the most powerful men.

The Black Virgin in Egypt

THE DUNG AFFIXED by Chris Ofili to his The Holy Virgin Mary had sensational effects all over the world. Although mothers are familiar with dung no matter whether they live in town OR country, city fathers who do not change diapers are reluctant to have much to do with dung personally, assigning such matters to their wives and other sanitation officials. Of course, farmers with livestock and those who use natural methods of cultivation are intimate with dung.

The mention of dung is certainly appropriate within the historical context of The Holy Virgin Mary scandal. Hebrew prophets were well aware of the fertilizing property of dung whether real or ideal: they called idols "dung"—all idols were dung except their own ark and its deposits.

And the Egyptians, whose sacred images were referred to as dung by the Hebrews, had good reason to appreciate the virtues of dung. They used dung as fertilizer to supplement the silt carried down to them by the Nile. Therefore, as we trace the movements of the Black Virgin, it shall behoove us to examine the issue of dung in Egypt.

First of all, the Black Virgin was know as Isis in Egypt. She was the Queen of all domains. She was understandably most popular as Goddess of the Nile; her great river, sometimes known as her husband Osiris, flowed through her black virgin soil, and much to the benefit of mankind: in Isis' heyday, her black virgin soil provided a living paradise on Earth. Osiris himself came and went; he was associated with the Underground Stream as god of the Other World, returning through his son Horus; but Isis was the First Mother and the Eternal Throne of Osiris.

The ancient Egyptians were expert irrigation-canal builders, and they did use dung as fertilizer. Although a great deal has changed since the good old days, especially in respect to religion, dung is still recognized in Egypt for its ancient virtue as a fertilizer; that clue to the travels of the Black Virgin beckons us to take advantage of an optional tour of the Nile, not quite the pretty cruise offered by the travel agencies.

Now that the Nile has been damned at Aswan to tame the flood in order to curb the broad feast-or-famine swings resulting from the natural cycle, chemical fertilizers must be employed; there is insufficient dung to make up for the lost silt. Critics of the Aswan High Dam complain of the lack of nutrients in the soil. They also claim that the silt-free water erodes barrages and bridge foundations, that it has caused coastal erosion of the delta, and that the reduction of flows has caused saline inundation from the Mediterranean resulting not only in the salty soil but also the loss of fish.

Furthermore, the artificial lake behind the Aswan dam has submerged and threatens to further submerge the ancient artifacts of one of the first organized states in human history, Nubia, and has run the Nubians, a black people who once ruled Egypt for over a century, off their land. Nubian women were famed for their beauty, an ideal beauty employed by artists as the model for certain black granite statues of Isis. Ironically and fortunately, the great temple of Isis at Philae in Nubia was removed to the island of Agilkia. The cult of Isis survived in Nubia to about the 6th century, long after she had been remodeled into a white virgin in Europe. Other monuments in Nubia have not been nor will they be so lucky. In fact, it seems Nubia has lost her attraction. Some Nubians now long for those ancient days, such as the day when the legendary Moses married a Nubian much to the dismay of his sister Miriam, the prophetess; perhaps not because

Miriam was a racist, but because the Kushite woman was a prophetess of Isis in direct competition with Miriam's own practice.

Yes, excremental side excursions can serve as food for thought and fertilizer for future growth. But let us remain in Egypt for a bit longer and travel back in time to the carnival, to the procession of shrines, accompanied by flutes, tambourines, hand-clapping, dancing, singing, and, among many other things, to generous offerings of wine, beer, oil and milk—yet a vase of water takes precedence, whether it anoints the fore or aft of the precious ark. And here comes yet another ark, of Isis, bearing her king, who prays the prayer of all kings, for a single blessing: Eternal Life.

The sacred casket of Isis' consort Osiris is borne, on long staves passing through metal rings, by twelve black-cassocked disciples led by their pope. The pontiff wears the garment and carries the magic club of the first world hero, then prehistoric Hercules, the heroic Cave Man of the Stone Age who cleared the Way for civilization.

Every significant personage in our parade has his float staffed by a crew of priests and their pontiff. And what wonderful conveyances the floats are, over land, sea, and sky. We enjoy the fragrant beauty of the talented women everywhere to be seen, some of whose charms exceed the excellencies of Elizabeth Taylor in her Egyptian garb, eyes protected by blue eye-shadow.

But hold on: what is that "thing" in the boat over there? That beetle with hawk-wings pushing a ball of fresh dung before it? That beetle protected by the enveloping wings of two angels, Inspiration and Expiration, fanning the breath of Truth? That thing is Khepri, the dung-beetle form of the Sun-god creator, represented by a scarab emblem wherever life is expected to go on despite its travails and its seemingly final tragic conclusion.

Khepri is reputedly even older than the great Ra-form of the Sun-god. Khepri is the sunrise, the morning, the birth of a new day, the resurrection of the body. He is, therefore, very good news. The scarab beetle lays its egg in dung and then pushes it around until it becomes a ball from which the larva eventually emerges. The wet and warm ark of dung pushed around by the beetle was, to the Egyptians, analogous to the Sun pushed around the sky by a huge beetle.

But we must bring our option tour to a screeching halt; still, even in its brevity, our brief excursus into the culture of Egypt reveals that dung is not something to be scorned and set aside as obscene, disgusting and useless, but it is rather something to be examined for its highest and best uses, a material to be pushed ahead as our own globe hurtles at an astonishing relative speed through black virgin space. Even though he might have been unconscious of his motive, perhaps that is why Chris Ofili shellacked a clump of dung on his painting The Holy Virgin Mary. We should keep that in mind during our future excursions into excremental culture.

Primitive Vestiges and Anal Therapy

IF WE ARE TO TOLERATE THE VESTIGES of "primitive" religions represented in Chris Ofili's post-modern painting, The Holy Virgin Mary,' in order to keep conscience clean we should give some brief regard to the post-modern psychoanalytic return to the Primitive, at least in reference to elephant dung and associated matters. We therefore note a reference thereto by French psychoanalyst Jacques Lacan.

According to Sherry Turkle in her book *Psychoanalytic Politics*, Lacan raised the elephant dung issue before a MIT audience in 1975. He said he was reasonably certain in his capacity as an analyst that man does have an interior: the evidence he found for that interior was the presence of excrement. Lacan claimed that man is the only animal who does not instinctively know what to do with his dung, except the dog, who is also civilized and, therefore, also encumbered by dung. Lacan said that elephant dung does not occupy much space even though it is reasonable to expect it to require, considering the size of the animal producing it, enormous accommodations. Then he equated civilization with excrement. He remarked that it would take a long time for people to understand what he was talking about. His audience thought he was delirious and senile—he was 72 at the time.

Lacan must not have been familiar with the production capacity of elephants. Thai researchers have recently generated electricity from elephant-dung natural gas. An elephant produces 88-110 lbs. of dung per day, enough to produce cooking gas for a family of three, or it can be used as feedstock for an electric generator. But the cost is not cheap.

The minimum price of construction of a fermentation pit, pipeline and storage tank is around $800 and a generator that could use the gas costs around $2,667. The Thai ministry responsible for the project plans to release a report promoting use of the method nationwide, especially in the North and the Northeast where most of the country's domesticated elephants are found and the problem of how to dispose of the elephants' waste is most acute. -(AP)- Bangkok, Thailand, February 23, 2000.

Despite that contradiction to Lacan's hypothesis, to be fair we shall render a few extractions from the ancient literature in his support or his general position.

Elephants themselves have long been associated with divinity and wisdom. The elephant is the Indian dragon with the snake of wisdom for its proboscis. It is the great god Indra's indispensable steed or vehicle, called Airavata, one of his necessary auspicious signs, equally important if not more so than his chakra, jewel, queen, treasure and horse. Airavata. meaning "produced from the ocean", came from the Ocean of Milk stirred up at the Creation. He is a cloud-white or milky-white elephant. Wherefore wars were once waged for the mere possession of a white elephant, and their images were placed as capitals on pillars and worshiped.

Celestial elephants have wings and can fly like clouds. It has long been known that they, as does the Chinese dragon, bring luck and abundance down to Earth. In fact, elephants fertilize the Earth Goddess: therefore she loves the sound of approaching elephants. Furthermore, so powerful is the fresh dung of white elephants that an ancient prescription for barrenness provides that infertile women stand in it for one hour prior to intercourse with their husbands.

Moreover, since the elephant is a royal vehicle, elephant dung may be a sign of the coming of a great lord. For instance, consider the myth about the birth of Buddha. His mother, Mayadevi, fell asleep and dreamed. Bodhisattva, in the form of a white elephant descended from a golden mountain, circled her bed clockwise three times, smote her right side, then entered her womb. A brahmin, upon hearing her account , prognosticated, "Thou shalt have a son. If he dwells in the house he will become a king, a universal monarch if he leaves the house and goes forth from the world, he will become a Buddha, a remover in the world of the veil of ignorance."

Incidentally, lest we become too grave about this matter, The Mesopotamians had a sense of humor concerning the droppings of the great elephant: their account of the Flood relates how the elephants stood on one side of the Ark, nearly causing it to roll over and capsize by weight of their excretions.

Those examples alone, and there are many more in the literature, should suffice to support Dr. Lacan's statement asserting the positive relation of dung to the advance of civilization. Nonetheless, a few more references will reinforce our case.

Take for instance, the first anthropological evidence of capitalism: it seems a primitive North American tribe gorged themselves to speed up their production of ordure, then baked it in the sun and stored it for future consumption in case of dire need.

Also consider the fact that, among the Kujamaat Diola of Senegal, certain individuals used to defecate in secret places in the bushes, then adopted the leavings as their personal totems or animated doubles. And note that an Africa sacred object might be worthless in itself: it is merely the means of communication. For a descendant of Nigerian elephant hunters, that object might very well be a clump of shellacked elephant dung, a symbol of power intended to wish happy elephant hunting as well as the capture of many erotic butterflies by the illustrious sons of "The Holy Virgin Mary."

That which is called "primitive" is not as primitive as it sometimes seems when we proceed to analyze it, hence we return to psychoanalysis in hopes we may obtain good therapy during our excremental discourse.

The evolution of dung-consciousness in the developing child must be mentioned in our context. According to the psycho-anal lore, a child becomes intensely interested in its productions during the anal stage. According to the founding fathers of psychoanalysis, the child exchanges the wet, stinky and sticky product for clean dry sand, although he might pour water in the sand or show a predilection for mud. That product is, in turn, traded for pebbles, rocks and marbles. Hard currency, jewels and precious metals might eventually follow. If a man has been raised properly, he will not want to touch dirty money: liquid currency is disgusting to him. Working capital must not be held in the form of cash in pocket or in bank accounts but must be fully vested in productive assets. A hygienically inclined man will prefer plastic cards, and have his digital statements handled by his accountants. However, he might often be involved in construction projects that leave petrified *dejecta* all over the land, such as buildings, roads, machines and other stools of power.

Several sorts of characters might emerge because of the different quirks of toilet training. A child might become an artist. Every true artist is a sort of rebel. The rebellious child might start his first savings account during the training process just to give himself the pleasure of squandering it as he pleases despite the best efforts of his parents. However, he might scorn savings altogether because his parents cherish the same.

On the other hand, because of some other accident of upbringing during the critical anal stage, a child might become an uptight tightwad, a constipated person who might know he belongs in analysis but does not want to pay for it; by the way, the Greek word for analysis means "to loosen up."

We have by no means exhausted the prospects of civilization and its discontents relative to the anal erogenous zone. Yet we can have comfort in knowing that the latest group therapy practice may provide a great deal of relief to the malcontents and the discontented. Two hour sessions are conducted while the group sits on toilets; the pioneering analyst got this idea from the customary practice of men in ancient Rome who sat for hours on public toilets chatting with each other while taking care of business. Naturally, this new anal therapy is being subsidized by the United States Government.

Indeed! The Surgeon General of the United States has defined mental illness as a mental state interfering with production and relationships. A man must achieve optimum productivity in our society in order to have fully productive relationships, yet his duty to consume and to maximize production may interfere with those relations. In any event, a healthy individual must make at least an adequate or "normal" contribution to the Gross National Product. Consumerism is the official state religion: continuous production is worshiped because of the manna that products supposedly contain, and because of the cathartic release of tension. Therefore the new anal therapy is conducive to the religion of consumption and production, and therefore merits the allocation of public funds.

It seems our society has resorted to a massive pantheistic idolatry. Mr. Lacan might not be so crazy and coprophilic as he seemed when he said civilization is excrement: a great deal of crap is now being frantically produced in developed countries just so people can get a bite to eat.

I Thought The Immortal Story Was About Me

IT WAS IN THE YEAR 2005 that I encountered Isak Dinesen's book of five fateful stories, *Anecdotes of Destiny*, in the 3-for-$2 cardboard boxes at Kafka's Kafé on South Beach, a block away from Al Capone's old hideout, the Clay Hotel. Selecting it from the haphazard collection in the cheap-books boxes was a gesture to the memory of my dear father. He loved her stories, highly recommending them to me in my youth.

After I read the 'The Immortal Story' in the small volume, I regretted choosing Dinesen's book instead of the dog-eared biographical sketches of saints, or the collection of famous short stories including Kafka's Metamorphosis. It seemed like the story was about me. I recalled that I, like Kafka, could not stand life at my fated home. Unlike him, I ran away at an early age and never returned – even so, like snails, we take the carapace with us. I had read about Kafka's absurd cockroach-like bug a dozen times, so I passed over Metamorphosis, even though the Absurd is relevant to my reverse metaphorical metamorphosis, from bookworm to man.

Not that I thought Dinesen's immortal novella was poorly written – quite to the contrary. Yet her description of greedy Mr. Clay's Jewish accountant, Elishama Levinsky, caused me to wince and reflect morbidly at length on my career as a bookkeeper and accountant, an occupation I took up when broke because Mary Anne in New Zealand said I would always have a job if I did so. To that extent I thought the author's account was about me, wherefore I took keen interest in it.

Heretofore I had thought of myself as an eccentric man, unique and undoubtedly original in many respects. Mind you that I am a frustrated book writer inasmuch as bookkeeping frustrates my utter transition from king's scribe to scribbling on my own account.

Now a novella is usually a moral tale. 'The Immortal Story' certainly pricked my conscience, and I felt destined to discover why that was so. For the life of me, the moral of the story was a mystery to me upon first reading. If only I could solve it, I felt, my chances for good fortune might be considerably improved. At least I would know my destiny and my fate – may writing seal my fate.

Since Dinesen was preoccupied with myths and symbols, I wondered, first of all, what meaning the substance, clay, might have in this everlasting myth? Jesus applied clay to the eyes of a blind man and he was healed: "He put a paste in my eyes, I washed, and I can see." Perhaps the Mr. Clay will provide us with some insight into the fundamental nature of human commerce. Man of course is made of clay. As Isaiah said to Yahweh, "For you hid your face from us, and gave us up to the power of our sins. And yet, Yahweh, you are our Father. we the clay, you the potter, we are all the work of your hand." Pots that serve their potter contain his treasures, valuables precious and useful to him. Could Mr. Clay, the mean old miser, be hoarding riches for the Lord? Clay can be pliable or brittle. Jeremiah lets us know that the House of Israel can be knocked down and built up again by the potter if he is displeased with its shape. Are we merely the Lord's toys? According to Job, such maxims and retorts are "proverbs of ash, your retorts, retorts of clay." Furthermore, on the subjected of unfired clay, "What then of those who live in houses of clay. who are founded on dust? They are crushed as easily as a moth, one day is enough to grind these to powder."

Dinesen gives us scant description of the rich nabob. Mr. Clay is apparently clay fire-hardened in the forge of commerce. He was the foremost nabob of Canton, quite naturally a mean man despite his prodigious means - in sum, one million guineas on hand. "A million pounds, that million pounds is me myself. It is my days and years, it is my brain and my heart, it is my life," he once proclaimed. He was a miser, an iron-hard man when not a stony figure. He was single and he liked to be alone. He once said that being stranded on a desert island must be a good thing: "a highly pleasant thing, I should say, to be all by yourself on an island, where nobody can possibly intrude on you." He had deliberately ruined his partner – a genteel Frenchman who had been weakened by "unlucky speculations" – leaving the partner on the streets to commit suicide. The partner's family disappeared from sight – Mr. Clay took over their fine house. He was about seventy years of age and suffering from a painful condition when we pick up the story. The old stone-man's successful career as a nabob made him feel omnipotent, to the extent of wanting – at the ripe old age of seventy and lacking an heir for his fortune – to make an old-sailor's tale, the Immortal Story, come true. And he did just that, and the truth was the death of him, so that the story, which spelled out his fate, might be true for others.

Could Mr. Clay be, besides a clay pot, a philosopher's stone or a touchstone? Might he be a stone that, when stricken by the magic wand, would flow forth fortune in golden terms?

"For I will pour out water on the thirsty soil, streams on the dry ground. I will pour my spirit on your descendants, my blessing on your children. They shall grow like grass where there is plenty of water, like poplars by running streams," quoth Isaiah.

As for Elishama Levinsky, only El knows why Dinesen named him Elishama, meaning the voice crying out in the wilderness "whom El hears" (elishama). We find several Elishamas in scripture, but Elishama, scribe to King Jehoiakim, is the most likely source for the namesake given Mr. Clay's bookkeeper.

In 1975, 250 clay seals were found about 44 miles southwest of Jerusalem. among them were the seals of four biblical figures.

“Elishama, Servant of the king”, was formally inscribed on one clay seal. Jeremiah’s famous first scroll, listing all the evils Yahweh had in mind for wayward Jews if they did not repent forthwith, was deposited in Elishama’s office in the royal palace for safekeeping, after it had been read aloud to the people in the Temple. The king was duly informed. the scroll was retrieved from Elishama’s office and read to the king, who, in turn, burned each section of the scroll after it was read. Wherefore Yahweh caused Jeremiah to dictate a similar scroll to Baruch, adding to the original threats a statement that King David’s throne would be vacated, and King Jehoiakim’s corpse would be tossed out into the heat of the day and chill of the night, and all the disasters listed in the destroyed scroll would be brought down on the entire people of Judah. Fair enough.

Elishama Levinsky had washed up by chance in Canton, bleached out, without ambition nor desire nor fear for the loss of anything except security and solitude. Mr. Clay had employed him for seven years. Elishama was known by the other accountants in his office as Ellis Lewis, a name he had assumed not because he was on the run like other expatriates around Canton, but rather to cover up the crimes committed against him during his peregrinations as a proverbially persecuted Jew. He had fled Poland with other Jews after the 1848 Pogrom. He was, wrote Dinesen, "a lost and lonely child, wholly in the hands of chance, who had lived through sufferings in Frankfurt, Amsterdam, London, and Lisbon." An old man who had died during the flight from Poland had given young Elishama a piece of paper upon which had been written in Hebrew several prophecies of Isaiah. The child carried it in a red bag hanging from his neck for some years. By chance an Italian bookkeeper in London took Elishama in, taught him double-entry bookkeeping and how to read and write words.

The heroine of the story, Virginie, the daughter of the French partner whom Mr. Clay had ruined, referred to Elishama as "a small rat." Quite naturally Elishama had his redeeming qualities, if we want to call them that. For instance, his early experience with horse-trading caused him to sympathize with women. he was the perfect person to negotiate the purchase of a woman in order to make the immortal story come true for Mr. Clay. As for other animals, he also liked birds because they reminded him of women. But the possession of goods was not Elishama's reason for being. He derived a great deal of comfort from the contemplation of the concept of the numerical series, but he treasured more than anything his solitude.

"One passion he had, if passion it may be called - a fanatical craving for security and for being left alone. In its nature this feeling was akin to homesickness or to the instinct of the homing pigeon. His soul was concentrated upon this one request: that he might enter his closet and shut his door, with the certainty that here no one could possibly follow or disturb him."

His dark room was modestly furnished, with a table, a chest, two chairs, and the sofa upon which he slept – only the sofa was his, such was his despite for possessions:

"Elishama, who despised the goods of this world, passed his time from morning tell night among greedy and covetous people, and had done so all his life. This to him was as it should be. He understood to a nicety the feelings of his surroundings, and he approved of them. For out of those feelings came, in the end, his closet with the door to it, If the world's desperate struggle for gold and power were ever to cease, it was not certain that his room or this door would remain. So he used his talents to fan and stir up the fire of ambition and greed in people around him. He particularly fanned the fire of Mr. Clay's ambition and greed, and watched it with an attentive eye."

Mr. Clay liked to have Elishama read the trader's old account books in the evenings before bedtime to distract him and help him fall asleep. One evening, Mr. Clay, bored with the historical transactions of his enterprise, asked his accountant if he had heard anything about the existence of another sort of account, an accounting besides financial accounting, accounts of human events and experiences. in a word, stories. Did Elishama know any stories? No, replied Elishama. But upon further consideration of his client's needs, or rather his client's greed and his need to fan it to retain his accounting position, he recited the prophetic verses of Isaiah that he had carried out of Poland in the red bag around his neck.

In sum, sufferings of one order or another are pleasantly relieved by the Lord in the end. "And sorrow and sighing shall flee away."

Mr. Clay was a realistic man. He did not like the prophecies because they appertained to something that did not exist. to wit, the future. At which point he proceeded to tell Elishama the one true story he did know, the immortal story, believed to originate somewhere very near the Cape of Storms and Good Hope. Elishama interrupted him, and proposed that he finish the story for Mr. Clay, for Elishama had also heard the tall tale, a tale told by every hopeful sailor in every port of call, a story that accounts for, in particular form, the universal wish for the relief of privation. In sum, a sailor is picked up by a childless rich man in a carriage and given a 5-guinea gold piece to come home with him, have dinner, and sleep with a beautiful woman in a luxuriously appointed bedroom. As a consequence of the mating, the rich man might have an heir to his fortune.

Of course the story is untrue, explained Elishama, much to his patron's chagrin: It is a matter of wishful thinking. We have a tendency to vividly imagine the things we are deprived of and to concoct stories about the satisfactions expected. For instance, financial schemes take advantage of our cravings and invariably promise more than they actually pay.

Wishful thinking did not suit Mr. Clay's disposition. after all, he was virtually King of Canton, an empire as far as he was concerned.

"The story shall become reality," Mr. Clay proclaimed, and he persuaded Elishama to make it so. And to what end? "I have not troubled to look for a hand into which I might like to deliver my possessions," said he, "for I know that no such hand exists in the world. But it has, in the end, occurred to me that it might give me pleasure to leave them in a hand which of I self cause caused to exist."

His possessions, he thought, would be the only part of him surviving his demise. His accountant was to spare no expense in arranging for the affair's accoutrements: the gold piece, the bedroom setting, and, among other things, the most expensive item of all, the fateful woman. She would be, by some twist of fate, the very daughter of the partner ruined by Mr. Clay. Of course he would play the part of the rich old man, venture out in the carriage and pick up a lucky sailor off the streets.

As far as Elishama was concerned, greed for the things of this world is madness. Mr. Clay "had always been mad," in his opinion. Yes, Elishama believed that "the old man was undoubtedly mad" in his desire to make every sailor's dream, of being paid in gold for a night with a beautiful woman, come true, not to mention the miser's proverbial wish for an heir to preserve his fortune. However, wrote Dinesen, Elishama "was not sure whether, to a man with one foot in the grave, the pursuit of a story was not a sounder undertaking than the pursuit of profit. Elishama at any time would side with the individual against the world, since, however mad the individual might be, the world in general was sure to be still more hopelessly and wickedly idiotic." Of course one must die when the story comes true, just as it would for Mr. Clay.

Now, then, during the telling of this immortal tale, the superstitious reader, namely me, by virtue of déjà vu and universal vanity, gets the distinct impression that he is a participant in the perennial plot. Indeed, the ancient doctrine of eternal recurrence of all plots comes to mind. In this case, the keeper of many books might conclude that Mr. Clay, at the moment of truth (death) is at once born again to relive the story of his life again, and then again *ad infinitum*. Likewise for the rest of the stereotypical characters, whose different times of birth and death require an infinite number of parallel universes to coincide, that the immortal story may be told again and again to the end of all times. Finally, we realize that the immortal story, notwithstanding modern copyright laws, is repeated with impunity. in fact it must be repeated, for it is sort of a law unto itself.

You are so vain, I told myself, that you thought the story was about you, and in fact it was about me. I did not get the drift at first, but it eventually dawned on me that I am not the eccentric character I thought I was, for there are an infinite number of characters just like me. So many captains of ships bring sailors from deserted islands into virgin ports, each sailor bearing a big pink shell he picked up there, which he leaves with the bookkeeper of the rich man who dies when the immortal story comes true. When the accountant puts his ear to the pink shell, it jumbles the story into roaring surf, advising all who fight riptide and undertow in vain, "To thine own story be true." Of course the rare accountant who loves to write must render a full account of it, and after the story is told, nary a sound shall remain for the conch to jumble. Only the Voice of the Silence remains for that particular cast of characters. and only by listening to that voice may they know themselves.

I recalled the pink conch offered to me in Negril, Jamaica, far from Dinesen's Africa. My current isolation resembles a deserted island, and I have high hopes that the captain will sail into port any day now. I often visit a marina in my neighborhood and imagine myself in possession of a luxury yacht with a buxom blonde as my first mate—a German maiden will do very well if a noble Frenchwoman cannot fit the bill of lading. When Dinesen's sailor was stranded on a desert island, he dreamed of having the ark he would inevitably inherit. it was not a big ship, but rather a sloop, "not more than five lastages long." Someday soon I may fulfill the Delphic injunction, and know myself.

"You are so vain," I told my alter ego. "you thought the story was about you, and in fact it was about me." You see, my father had recommended Dinesen's works to me, with that stern authoritative tone of his, before he died. I had perused her Gothic tales, but I did not care for her subtle obscurations or her fatalism, for I still wanted to make something of myself as the master of my own fate. I did not get the drift of her Immortal Story now that I encountered it in South Miami Beach, but it would eventually dawn on me that I am not the eccentric character I thought I was, for there are an infinite number of characters essentially like me, symbolically speaking, notwithstanding the accidental attributes.

So many captains of ships bring sailors from deserted islands into virgin ports, each sailor bearing a big pink shell or conch he picked up somewhere, which he leaves with the bookkeeper of the rich man who dies when the immortal story comes true.

When the accountant puts his ear to the pink shell, it jumbles the story into roaring surf, advising all who fight riptide and undertow in vain: To thine own story be true.

Naturally the rare accountant who loves to write must render a full account of it, and after the story is told, nary a sound shall remain for the conch to jumble; only the Voice of the Silence remains for that particular cast of characters; and only by listening to that voice shall they know themselves.

I recall again the pink conch offered to me in Negril, Jamaica. My current isolation resembles a deserted island, and I have high hopes that the captain will sail into port any day now. I often visit a marina in my neighborhood, and imagine myself in possession of a luxury yacht with a bosomy blonde as my first mate; a German maiden will do very well if a noble Frenchwoman cannot fit the bill of lading. When Dinesen's sailor was stranded on a desert island, he dreamed of having the ark he would inevitably inherit; it was not a big ship, but rather a sloop, "not more than five lastages long." Now I realize why the poor man in Negril was so angered by my rejection of the pink conch: I could have saved both of us from bad times if only I had purchased it and put it to my ear.

Yet I still did not fully remember myself after I read The Immortal Story. My version of self-revelation was flawed, as if I were at present an imposter if not a crackpot. Someday soon I may fulfill the Delphic injunction, and know myself. Might I, in microcosm, very well be, if not a bug, or a baked clay artifact, the symbolic stone in need of being stricken by the rod? Does the enigmatic archetype of Mr. Clay and the like stand for the black-emerald foundation Stone under the Temple that plugs the waters of the Abyss? Is that not the very stone which King David dared to raise to have a look into the awful pit, causing him to be duly affrighted, and to cast into the Abyss a clay shard inscribed, 'YHWH', lest the world suffer another great deluge?

Although I am more of a storyteller than an accountant, Elishama (the man "Whom God Hears"), the miser's lonely accountant, and I have our similarities.

Elishama's comparison of women with birds is perfectly understandable. I was given to concentrate on the features of the human body during my dancing days, particularly the delicate structure of the bones of the female's upper body. I was wont to say, "Women come from the sky; men come from the muck."

As for rats, I may be rat-like but I am not a little rat nor am I a mouse. Of course I would not mind being called a mouse by a sympathetic friend, for I am told the mouse is an ancestor to the human race—the little creature had to dance around at night without disturbing huge animals, thus was an extraordinary demand created for keen eyesight, intelligence, agility, and so on.

I took up dancing for about twenty hours per week when I was keeping books; both dancing and bookkeeping require a great deal of counting. I have become a fat rat after I stopped dancing. Fat though I may be, I am no pack rat. I do not ferret away property in secret accounts, at least not on my own account. I respect property but I do not want a lot of it, hence my client's property was safe in my hands. As for money, well, I admit it, I have been lonely for dollars from time to time, but not lonely enough to steal it, which seems to be the thing to do at all levels of society nowadays.

Elishama liked to hole up in a closet. That makes good sense. I have holed up in modest quarters most of my life. You see, I was most interested in my own personal security because of my insecure childhood. The loss of my mother, my first stepmother, and my foster home initiated me into an insecure life. My second stepmother's hatred for me prompted me to leave my third home when I was thirteen. That was risky indeed, but I eventually acquired a habit of holing up somewhere and taking very few risks, even the more so after I quit drinking.

My aversion to risk did not, however, prevent me from being foolish and rash; how would a young fool know when he is being young and foolish? Wanting security and the family I never had, I managed to force myself on two women and ruin two marriages; I did not have the slightest idea of what a real family was.

Of course it takes two to tango; therefore I refuse to take all the blame. Badly burned by my passions and bad habits, I eventually foreswore everything but coffee and crawled into holes and cracks in the walls here and there, where I was happy enough with myself as long as I had something to read and could afford the rent.

I eventually gave up television and movies and stopped reading everything except financial statements and business reports for quite awhile. Once inside my quarters, I resented the slightest disturbance, even the peep of a mouse not to mention telephone calls.

There exists in me yet another resemblance to Elishama. If my family tree carved on the huge stone under the castle is true, I, like Elishama, have a Semitic strain, although you might not know it unless you were a Jewish mother or a Nazi. My Semitic rivulet runs all the way back to Jeremiah; who, according to my family tradition, did not get stoned to death in Egypt but managed to find security in the British Isles. Although Elishama was fanning the fires of ambition and greed in Mr. Clay, he was not portrayed as greedy himself, except for his pathetic need for basic security.\No, I certainly am not Mr. Clay. I am more like Elishama. I do have some Hebrew clay in my grind; unlike Mr. Clay, I am dirt poor. I am a friendly and somewhat silly sort of fellow. I love the world so much that I laugh at it daily, and even the more so when that little gray songbird with the long tail sings his aria at the bus stop in the morning.

No doubt Baroness Karen Christentze von Blixen-Finecke was laughing from time to time when she wrote The Immortal Story. She adopted the Hebrew namesake, Isak, meaning, "one who laughs." My own sense of humor is so dry that people think I am as depressed as any miser or his accountant. Not so. And I am passionate, never stony.

Like Mr. Clay, I have hoarded my resources, but not because I wanted them in themselves, say, in the form of gold. Nor did I really want a luxury yacht, at least not until of late. I wanted to buy time to write my story, a golden ark no doubt, one that would carry soulful seeds to the realization of my most grandiose dream; nothing less than the salvation of humankind, which would naturally include me. Indeed, I wrote of writing myself to death to that altruistic end.

No, greedy merchant I am not: I kept books for my keep, counting the treasure but never wanting its burdens. I am willing to accept myself whatever I might be. Still I want much more than my present worth.

Mind you that I have cause to believe that I am a reality, and not a work of fiction: I can tell stories about myself, therefore I exist.

I happen to remember a few accounts of myself in the context of what I picked up along the wayside and developed under the influence of my race. One rather vague story appertains to my heritage, gleaned from various sources including the films of corpse-filled trenches, venereal disease, and marijuana madness shown to boys at Clay School, a Topeka, Kansas grammar school, where we did the Hop, and where a voluptuous sixth-grade farmer's daughter got pregnant and married.

And I remember my father's frequent references to his persecution by Masons and "the people with low foreheads"; my grandmother's conversion to Catholicism, her worship of the bishop, her forbiddance of the word "Jew" being said in her presence; and, among other things, my own persecution as a child and my hitchhiking exile, at age thirteen, from the Heartland of America to the Great Lakes and beyond.

You see, I was once a troubled boy, a juvenile delinquent who admired Black Beard the Pirate and Al Capone, who as a precocious boy of eight and nine had read the Wizard of Oz, Oliver Twist, The Three Musketeers, The Hunchback of Notre Dame, and Moby Dick. I set sail for the streets of Chicago, where I slept in bus and train stations when I did not have the price of a movie ticket. I scavenged food and scrounged small change with other runaways. I idolized the public Madonna in a church in the Loop. And when Our Lady of Sorrows did not seem to respond, I unwittingly placed on my pedestal any woman who foolishly said "yes," beginning with a bisexual, 17-year-old stripper for the Outfit in Cal City, hoping that I might find salvation from alienation within women instead of me. Experience helped fashion me into a beer-guzzling bookworm; and then, to overcompensate, into a teetotaler with an extremely dry sense of humor and a sizable account payable to society. I became a mystical atheist who would fain avoid the bill and become a monk if only a monk who would not have to force faith in the First Father in Heaven nor obey His infallible popes on Earth. I have a growing sense of debt and gratitude that I survived, for I do love life, and I shall endeavor to pay my debt with minted coin when my story comes true.

Little did I know that I would become a lowly bookkeeper: I imagined that I was on my way to Tobacco Road and the likes of Tammy when I ran away from home, but I was by chance dropped off in Chicago by the car thief and fireworks smuggler who picked me up at a Missouri gas station.

I cut my teeth in the Windy City, and wandered on to other cities. I took up several kinds of blue-collar and clerical jobs along the way: busboy, hospital orderly, X-ray dark-room technician, quality control clerk, drill press and lathe operator - - the union guys got me fired because I turned out too many screws.

And then I was a freight claims clerk in the legal department of the Milwaukee Road. Among other bureaucratic duties at the railroad, I and the fellow next to me added up the same lists of lost or damaged items twice. We did not have adding machines, so one of us would add the lists from the top down; the other would add them from the bottom up. Perchance calculating totals gibed with my destiny as a controller. Controllers used to be 'contrarotulators.' They were responsible for making sure transactions were added up twice, but on separate rolls: the totals on the rolls were compared against each other to make sure they were identical.

The Chief Clerk, pursuant to a Directive from the Controller, insisted that the totals be identical, right down to the last digit; after all, a minor difference one way or the other, he explained, could be the net result of major mistakes, unless the difference in digits added up to nine, and even then the mistake might be consequential.

A banker once explained to me many years later that his bank was out of balance one day by ninety dollars; the difference was the net result of mistakes amounting to around two million dollars, and the mistakes were never found to be corrected. I also discovered during my accounting career that it is unlawful to spend a million dollars mistakenly credited to your account by a bank. But it was supposedly all right to keep a double payment from a private company. An accounts payable manager screamed at me that it was impossible for her to make a double payment of $150,000 to my company's account. I asked the boss what to do, and he said he would hold the money in trust. It was still in trust when the company went bankrupt two years later. I remember when a Wall Street company paid another company $350,000 bill three times after hiring an incompetent controller off the golf course; that overage was held by the boss, posted to a current account payable on demand. When the federal government overpaid another company I worked for, by $725,000, with one of those little computer checks you have to rip the edges off the envelope to get at, the boss said to return it although we did not have enough money to make the payroll; I called the disbursement officer; after that, the government paid us quickly whenever I called him.

In retrospect, my job handling freight claims in Chicago as a young man seems more worthy of a would-be writer than my bookkeeping jobs. However that may be, I wore pleated- and cuffed-pants, silver- and gold-embroidered vests over fancy cuff-linked shirts with flared sleeves, silk cravats in big gold rings, and felt fedoras. Moreover, I was an esteemed member of the Brotherhood of Railway Clerks. I was credited with revolutionizing the filing system by stacking the files flat instead of standing them on edge in long rows. I still have a knack for filing, which sometimes calls for standing files on edges or ends as well as flat-stacking: for instance, I showed the manager at Kafka's how to stand the books on end in the cheap-books cardboard box so customers could finger through them without making a mess of it. Coincidentally, that is how I happened to run across Dinesen's book of fateful stories the other day.

Anyhow, little did I know during my railroad days that my wife, at one time a Federal Reserve check-clearing clerk, would go to work for W. Clement Stone's Combined Insurance Company and decide to dump me in Chicago; perhaps she was influenced by the Think And Grow Rich, Success Through A Positive Mental Attitude, and The Success System That Never Fails culture of W. Clement Stone and Napoleon Hill: my father had told me that a man who lets his wife work is looking for trouble. I loved her dearly, and the divorce almost killed me. And little did I know that I would leave Chicago and become a freight claims clerk for a private company in New York as well as a weekend hippie and student actor, or that I would do some night clerking at hotels on Miami's South Beach, wind up with a Jewish American Princess in Manhattan for a mad passionate week, and then move on to Hawaii, where I would by chance or providence meet Mary Ann from New Zealand, who caused me to learn bookkeeping and take a job in Accounts Payable, and then become a controller. Nor did I know that I would get a job in Kona as the right-hand man of a German wheeler-dealer and marry a Portuguese-Hawaiian savings and loan teller. I loved her, but I was glad to get back to bachelorhood, yet always hoping she might want me to come home some day.

And then, afraid that I would die in paradise without accomplishing much, I returned to New York to do it all over again from scratch, taking up bookkeeping and dancing, counting each step with a vengeance. As for writing, I managed to avoid wordsmithing until, when on the verge of relative success, a wave of nostalgia swept me back to Hawaii, to invest my savings in solitary research and writing brilliant essays, then to return to return to the Mainland again, this time to Kansas City of all places, nearly broke, fearful that I would miss something, namely my life, and then on to Miami, at the brink of the Abyss, and in Miami I encountered a Pink Conch on the A bus, and Isak Dinesen's The Immortal Story in the cheap-books box.

Ah, the good old days! I even recall the bad old days as good old days nowadays. No, I did not wear the accountant's garb at work, but I played the part of an in-house accountant well enough; that is, a conservative Dinesenian accountant. I handled the accounts well enough as well, and affected a penchant for organization and overt obedience to generally accepted principles. Still, I always knew I was not really an accountant nor was I a "mediocre" organization man. I certainly was not cut out to be a lowly bookkeeper. Please! I would ask, do not introduce me as "the bookkeeper"! At least call me "an accountant," and not my" accountant, for I imagined that I was independent; and I was in fact independent of certification, which made me more useful to the liberal client than the socialist public.

No, ma'am, I was definitely not the accounting type of person at heart. I was the creative type and everybody knew it, especially after I invited them to watch me prance across stages in tights or listen to me sing my renditions of 'I Fall To Pieces', 'The Lady in Black', 'Purple Rain', and a hundred and forty-one other songs in my repertoire. The outside CPAs would sometimes joke around and call me "the creative accountant." Notwithstanding my radical political profusions from time to time—something I learned from the FBI's anti-communism manual as a child—I was loyal to the bottom line and strove to strike a balance between right and left. I am a welfare capitalist at heart: it is, you know, quite profitable to treat people well - people who treat me right are righteous; they're all right, because they treat me right.

As for creative accounting in the ordinary sense of the phrase, I did not cook the books or keep two or three sets of them with different totals, nor did I help executives plunder corporations. Indeed, I perceived myself as the Lord High Chancellor or King's Conscience; someone who would not put up with any sort of unethical business, such as the fudging of numbers and capitalization of expenses and taking of bribes. By the way, I was unaware of Lord High Chancellor Francis Bacon's impeachment: I really can't say if I would have followed in his footsteps if I had known about his fees—King James wondered what people expected but bribery since he did not pay his high officials salaries. If I were a virtual bookkeeper, I once thought, then I was an English bookkeeper, for the ethics of English bookkeepers were once far superior to the scruples of certified American accountants! Why, even Mary Shelley, in Frankenstein, mentioned the "noble bookkeeper", for whom there was no higher art than bookkeeping - who needs the liberal arts when you have the business bible at hand? There is no hypocrisy in double-entries provided the books are perfected balanced.

Allow me to repeat myself to make myself perfectly clear: I was not what people sometimes called me, “the numbers man.” I was really a writer, actor, singer and dancer behind the numbers. In fine, an artist, and not the calculating worm in the back office behind the restrooms. Lowly worm that I was in terms of status, I warranted a private office, somewhere out of the way, the farther away from the front offices, the better. The top executives of several firms gave me a back office or one down the hall to protect themselves from their financial statements and my jeremiads thereupon. Mind you, I liked the back offices although I often complained that they are briar patches. I felt as snug as a bug in the last one: I loved its privacy, its distance from authority, its closeness to the restrooms. And when I felt expansive and opened my door, the proximity of my office to the employee dining room pleased me greatly, for I enjoyed chatting with the workers of the world when I was not counting the boss's money.

Incidentally, since I was someone who realized that the old overseers were fools for being cruel to slaves, I fancied myself as a humane socialist (not a moral fanatic) whenever I had to don my Human Resources hat.

Several of my bosses said I was "much more than a bookkeeper." They wanted to have me up front, conferring on strategies, hanging out in meetings, flying around the country troubleshooting and the like; but I eventually wanted to be left alone in the back office so I could concentrate on the books and analyze the numbers. While doing so, I often felt like a financial desert prophet. I liked to deliver the financials to the executives along with predictions of doom, which of course was inevitable unless certain steps were immediately taken to conserve resources or curb theft, curtail expenses, increase revenue, acquire loans and investments, and so on. Deficit spending was a mortal sin in my conservative black book of accrued balances. If a corporation could not so organize labor as to minimize expenses to its customers while paying labor decent wages and providing a fair return to investors and owners,

I figured it ought to be dissolved instead of being allowed to run up bills everywhere. As for my own budget, my sole objective was to save up enough money to buy the leisure time to retire to libraries where I would of course read and write books.

All the while I sincerely believed that I would become one of the greatest writers the world would ever know. I successfully pretended to be a bookkeeper, accountant and corporate comptroller, but I was in reality a natural born creative thinker and literary artist at heart. I avoided getting stepped on by the lords of land and business. I saved up for years and years, then, one day I up and quit my job and took up writing alone. I mean very alone: without even the benefit of tobacco, booze, and other diversionary drugs except caffeine.

Others and even I might say that I blundered, and at least I did not have as bad a time of it as the British did in Crimea. Indeed, I thought I had made a terrible mistake at the time, but I insisted on persisting in my vanity against my will to survive. Lo and Behold, I was offered the job of my dreams shortly thereafter, an offshore job on an island banana republic enjoyed by tax evading money laundering, pirates of sorts. A friend said the Devil was afoot.

I feared success self-defined. By virtue of an incredible act of virtual suicide, I turned down power aplenty; two paid vacations annually to anywhere in the world; a salary invisible to the IRS, exempted from foreign taxes by special dispensation of the prime minister; pilot's training and access to a small plane; access to wealthy people from all over the world. What especially alarmed me about the deal was all those goodies were to be had with a tourist visa and the naked promise of a prime minister. So I headed west to pursue my ideal career, to be a bookworm instead of a bookkeeper.

After all, according to the occupational preference tests I took many years ago, I was conditioned to be a wordsmith, not a bookkeeper. I would also be happy as a professor, lawyer, bookstore manager, public relations executive, and hairdresser. Crunching numbers was dead last on my preference list; you will find me with the artistic types at preferential cocktail parties. I took up bookkeeping because I was flat broke. Mary Ann said I would always make a living if I learned how to do the books. I rose rapidly from accounts payable to keeping the general ledger and cranking out financials and performing other duties associated with being a glorified bookkeeper, accounting manager, and corporate controller, aka comptroller.

Elishama managed to keep his job by fanning the fires of ambition and greed in his clients. But I can happily say that my clients have been more generous than greedy. And they were ambitious: their fires did not need any fanning from me. They paid me well in current dollars. I wanted to write full time, so I eventually saved up enough money to live well below the poverty level, and quit my job. I wished I had a better place to live in, and a million dollars to boot, but I still deem myself rich at $7.50 per day to live on after exorbitant rent for my hovel in paradise. Nevertheless, I applied for an accounting job again because I wanted to rent a nice apartment from a Joshua Clay. A man flew down to Miami from St. Louis to interview me.

"You are no longer an accountant and business man. You are a creative writer and that is what you should be doing."

I explained that being a creative writer narrowed my employment opportunities down to a needle in a haystack, and that I could keep books just as well as I could write them.

"That's your problem. You must live with it."

So here I am, after many years as a faithful button-pusher and key-banger on the ten-key adding machine, typewriter keys and computer keyboards.

I dread more than ever the probability that I might be fully discarded by society despite my literary talents. The Hindus say the body is just a coat, but it is one I don't mind wearing for the time being. I might lose my hovel to gentrification, be tossed onto the street with the furniture I retrieved from the alley. I have no garret to go to, not to mention the condo that went for $45 million a few blocks away last week.

The very idea of not having a least a roof over my head and a toilet is abhorrent to my inculcated bourgeois sensibility. Who knows? I may bloom late, if that be my fate, and enlighten some small part of the world with a brilliant collection of stories, perhaps entitled, Accounts Payable, My Life Past Due.

If It's Brown Put It Down

I WAS ASTONISHED when a friend told me it was a damn shame that an elderly man such as me had been attacked on the street in front Crunch Fitness in South Miami Beach. I have never considered myself as elderly although as a child I thought I might be thousands of years old, so I resented people when they called me a little boy at my foster home in Muskogee. I was also astonished when Tanya, the manager at Crunch, presented me with a certificate for physical therapy to help with my back, which I wrenched when I threw the heavy man who jumped on me onto the sidewalk.

I was inclined to decline the gift because being independent is my forte: I am more afraid of being dependent than of death itself. But I accepted it because Tanya is beautiful and sincere, and I remembered the Polynesian custom of accepting a gift: failing to do so would insult the giver. One chief had actually spat upon the pots, pans and mirrors the white man had brought to the island and laid out on a blanket. "We have our own things," said the chief, which was to say, "F*** you haole."

I was unable to stand and walk for two days after the incident, but I am mobile once again. The training sessions with Phil at the fitness club, albeit painful, have been helpful. I am worried that I may wind up in a wheelchair or a walker, which for me would be worse than death. My birthfather hobbled along without a walker until his death at ninety because, he said, "After they give you a walker they want to warehouse you and take away your social security."

Yesterday I heard a woman screaming "Ayudame, ayudeme!" I went outside and looked in between the buildings. There she lay on the sidewalk beside her walker. That reminded me of the advertisement for the notification device in the ad that warns people it is disturbing because an elderly woman was at the bottom of the stairs with her laundry crying, "Please help me, I've fallen."

My elderly neighbor was not hurt badly, just a scraped knee. She refused my offer to call 911.She said she had Medicare, but had a terrible experience when an ambulance came on a previous occasion.

My back still hurt, she was heavy, and lifting her back onto her walker was difficult. I got her into the elevator and into her apartment after considerable fiddling with her big ring of keys because she had trouble remembering which was which so I had to try them all. I noticed the elevator did not have a safety mechanism to keep the door open in case someone tried to stop it from closing by thrusting their arm into while it was closing.

Her English was minimal, and my Spanish is pathetic. I guessed correctly that her first name is Maria. She laughed when I said all Hispanic women are called Maria. She called her daughter from her phone inside the apartment, and then told me her daughter was drunk at her birthday party and would not come to help. I cleaned and bandaged her scraped knee, then left her because she could move around, and she said she had a helper coming in the morning, but would call me if she was in trouble. I emailed Captain de Espriella for advice. He takes good care of our neighborhood. If only his chief were not so liberal it would be even better. He promised to have someone look in upon her the next day and to get her social services if she needed it, as she is hardly able to walk.

A neighbor of mine said that Maria does have a maid coming in every day except on Sunday, and on Sundays she tends to go outside for a walk and often falls down and it's very difficult to get her home. The whole thing seems to be a ritual. Then her building manager said the poor lady gets tipsy, and I recalled the first thing the woman had done when I got her home was to offer me a drink.

I may be thousands of years old myself, and I think I can remember the dinosaur days, yet my spirit always seems relatively young compared to eternity. My body is obviously coming undone, and rather suddenly at that. I do not want to look into mirrors anymore. No one is going to call me little boy again, that much is for sure, though now that I think of it again, I am still that little boy. I'm sure everyone knows what I mean though they might not admit it.

Oh how my back ached this morning! Maybe my mattress, which I retrieved from the alley ten years ago, is making matters worse. The quality of discards in the alleys is going down in South Beach so I may write an essay on whether that is a sign of advance or decline of the quality of life. Beds cost a fortune; if I spend my life savings on one, my fortune would be wasted because rich people are buying up properties, rents are going through the roof, and we expect to be evicted soon. I would try to sleep on the hard floor if it were not for the huge palmetto bugs that pass through from time to time no matter what kind of cockroach spray one uses.

The game is obviously almost over, I realized once again as I looked at the wall, the wall I call death. Hopefully I will hit it in my sleep during a sweet dream, and my body will be taken away and cremated after they find the notification card in my wallet advising to cremate right away. I apologize in advance for the odor causing my body to be found, because nobody will miss me enough to inquire in the first place, which is my own fault, of course, for in America everyone but God is to blame for their fate. I chose to be an independent, honest author instead of money-grubbing writer. Honesty does not pay in this country; when I do tell the truth, which can be rather complicated, I am called a liar.

Oh how I regret nobody will bother forgiving me for my sins, and that I am not the gentleman I should be. I have managed to disgust myself after listening to people demean me. Maybe I could figure out how to commit suicide on the Internet, I thought, put down a plastic sheet under the chair, or why not a plastic bag over my head? Well, I am not suicidal, my back hurts, but things are not really as bad as they seem....

I finally got up from my mattress sideways so as not to aggravate my back. At least that is a positive step, I thought, and I admitted to myself I am not a good philosopher because according to Socrates wise men gladly consider death as a matter of habit. The purpose of life, after all, is death. I resolved to try to think of something else in the interim since my procreative days have passed along with a great deal of foolishness.

I affirmed that it was going to be a very nice day. I resolved to stop feeling old, to go to the homeless folk library and use the fancy new computers to avoid my own truth by researching other people's problems. I stopped by the Burger King for their excellent Arabic coffee along the way, and as I was sitting there, a Hispanic woman wearing jewelry approached me and offered me her hash browns. She evidently thought that I am a poor old perhaps homeless man reading my book, which happened to be Karl Marx's account of the Paris Commune because I love French history and dream of visiting France because prophets are not recognized at home and French people are revolutionary.

It occurred to me that I may have looked destitute because I was wearing brown. My friend Betty Jane warned me, that when looking in the closet for clothes to wear, if they are brown, put them down. If she had known about this lady wearing jewelry, she probably would have advised me to go home with her.

No, I am not thousands of years old, after all. I am going to take all my brown clothes, given to me by bereaved or divorced women, and put them in the alley for the homeless people living there.

Interesting Italian Americans I Have Met

A TOUGH YOUNG FELLOW in Chicago named Dino was my roommate in a squalid apartment beside the elevated tracks in Chicago in 1959. He taught me to use Rit Dye to dye my hair jet black and then to slick it back with petroleum jelly. He had a big heart. He worked at a diner whose owner fired the waitress because she was pregnant, so he stole the money from the register one night and gave her half of it, putting the other half in our icebox. He cut himself, banged his head on the wall, and said he had been robbed. She talked. He was busted, the police came and got the money out of the icebox, and Dino was sent off to prison.

Another fellow I liked was Mario, an older man whom I hung out with at the pool halls. He had been a lieutenant for Al Capone. I could not get him to talk about the good old days. Maybe they were not so good. Maybe he did time in the joint. He said it was against the code to talk. He did tell me that it was necessary to kill someone to get into the Outfit so they would have something on you. I did not believe that. What did I know? I was all of 14-years old, having arrived in Chicago with fifty cents in my pocket two weeks after my 13th birthday. The only thing I did not like about him was he always wanted to trade girlfriends, a desire that I and the girls thought was revolting though we were otherwise liberal.

I had no experience except dish washing and needed better paying work. Mario got me an interview with Sam Giancana, who was running things back then. I heard Sam was a stone cold killer, but he was pretty smooth, I thought. We met in the back of a Rush Street lounge. He bought me a daiquiri. I asked him if it were true that applicants had to kill someone. He did not answer. He just said that I had been watched, and that I was not qualified for a job with the Outfit because I liked to tell stories. I had picked up that habit from my dad, who studied journalism and law after the war. Sam told me to learn how to run an adding machine, and sent me to an employment agency in the Loop.

Angelo was not so nice. I had a small one-bedroom apartment at a hotel on Clark and Diversey. The restaurant where I was bussing dishes paid me cash for the week and let me go and because I had pneumonia and was coughing all over the place. I ran into Angelo on the way home. He asked me if he could stay the night at my apartment because his mother had kicked him out, so I put him up on my living room couch. The only medicine I had was a half pint of whisky, which I drank and passed out. When I arose I felt better but I discovered that Angelo had stolen all my clothes and money. It was bitter cold outside. I wrapped myself in a blanket, went to a phone booth and called Anna, my teenage Italian girlfriend in Oak Park, who got some money out of her mother's purse and rescued me. I saw Angelo downtown about a year later. I naturally beat the hell out of him in broad daylight, and then hid in a huge basement cafeteria. Sam was right when he said I was being watched. A man in a trench coat and wearing a fedora walked up to me and got me out of the Loop as the cops closed in.

Many years later while hanging out at Wilson's on 79th Street in Manhattan, I often chatted with a smooth young man somehow related to the Gotti family. He claimed he was not involved in criminal activities, but he mentioned his outfit was getting paychecks from the World Trade Center for maintenance services although he never went to the site. He invited me to visit the family peepshow business in Times Square. I declined, but I did visit their huge nightclub nearby. There was some kind of mob trouble going on then. He was always with a bodyguard, a Russian man who showed me photographs of his pet tiger at his dacha on the Caspian Sea. He told me he had been a KGB officer posted in Hanoi, I think during the Vietnam War. His English was terrible. When I asked him what he did, he said he "killed people." My Italian acquaintance corrected him, telling him the correct thing to say was "security consultant." My Italian acquaintance was exceedingly polite. For example, I asked his girlfriend what kind of work she did. "Work?" she asked indignantly, and was about to tell me off, but he sternly commanded her to "have respect." He eventually offered me work handling cash transfers. I had taken Sam's advice long ago, had gotten fast on adding machines, became an accountant, but I did not apply for the job because Sam had also told me I was not cut out for organized crime, and to also avoid the legal form of it, the government.

The few interesting Italian Americans I happened to become acquainted with in my peculiar circumstance are certainly not representative of them all. I liked them anyway, except for the one that left me nude in subfreezing weather. I would like to beat the hell out of him again.

I Was A Crack Adding Machine Operator

SAM GIANCANA SAID I WAS A GOOD KID who talked too much to be a member of the Outfit when I applied to him for a job running numbers. He told me to see a man he knew at an employment agency downtown in the Loop for work. The man told me that if I learned how to operate a ten-key adding machine, I would always be able to get a job.

I soon became a crack ten-key adding machine operator, but I was really not the numbers man some people thought I was. I was really the writer, actor, singer, and dancer hiding behind the slews of numbers. In fine, I was an artiste, and not the calculating worm in the back office behind the restrooms. I fulfilled the role of an uncertified private accountant rather well. I handled the accounts, balanced the books, and affected a penchant for organization and overt obedience to generally accepted accounting principles. Still, I always felt like an impostor. In fact, I always knew I was not really an accountant, nor was I a mediocre organization man. Most of all, I was not cut out to be a lowly bookkeeper. Please! I would ask, do not introduce me as the so-called bookkeeper! At least call me an "accountant," and not "my accountant," for I imagined that I was independent. Incidentally, my creative streak and the absence of certification sometimes made me more useful to private enterprise than to the democratic republic.

No, ma'am, I was definitely not the accounting type of person at heart. I was a creative type, and the CPAs knew it, especially after I invited them to watch me prance across stages in tights or to listen to me sing my renditions of 'I Fall To Pieces', 'The Lady in Black', 'Purple

Rain', and other songs from my extensive repertoire. The outside auditors sometimes joked around and called me a "recreational accountant."

A certain attitude is required of those who count other people's money. Notwithstanding my radical political profusions, I was loyal enough to vested interests. On balance I strove to strike a balance between right and left. As a matter of fact, I am a welfare-capitalist at heart. I believe in the principle that a few of our founding slaveholders adhered to, that it is quite profitable to treat people well. I even wrote a little Blue's song in that vein, one that I liked to sing on payday: "People who treat me right are righteous, they're all right, because they treat me right..." By the way, Rap music accompanies monotonous posting best, and Beethoven is best for cranking financials.

As for creative accounting in the ordinary sense of the phrase, I did not cook the books or keep two or three sets of them with different totals, nor did I help executives plunder corporations. Indeed, I perceived myself as the Lord High Chancellor or King's Conscience; someone who would not put up with any sort of unethical business, such as the fudging of numbers and capitalization of expenses and taking of bribes.

Yes, I know, Lord High Chancellor Francis Bacon was impeached, but what we call bribes today were merely fees back then; King James asked what else people expected of his officials given the fact that he did not pay salaries. But my present sympathies are with the English Revolution. If I were a bookkeeper instead of an accountant, I would be an English bookkeeper, for the ethics of English bookkeepers were once far superior to the scruples of certified American accountants! Why, even Mary Shelley mentioned the "noble bookkeeper" in her Frankenstein, the bookkeeper for whom there was no higher art than bookkeeping - who needs the liberal arts when you have the business bible at hand? In any case, there is no hypocrisy in double-entries as long as the books are perfected balanced!

Lowly worm that I was, I warranted being closeted somewhere out of the way, the farther away from the front offices the better. The executives of several firms gave me either a back office or one way down the hall, to protect themselves from their financial statements and my jeremiads thereupon. I liked the back offices. I felt as snug as a bug in a rug in the last such office: I loved its privacy, its distance from authority, its proximity to the men's room, and the dirty window that provided me with a Midtown perspective on the grimy city. I used to gaze upon the street below, and imagine people fleeing the buildings like rats as IRS squad cars marked "Form 1099 Independent Contractor Enforcement Division" arrived.

I left my door open when I was in an expansive mood, for the proximity of my office to the little dining room pleased me greatly. I enjoyed chatting with the workers of the world when I was not counting the boss's money. I shan't forget the young fellow who ate a turkey sandwich in the dining room one day, yawned, and said to me, "We people are lazy," meaning, of course, black folk. "Nonsense," I said, "we white people laid that on you. You ain't lazy, my boy, you just ate yourself some turkey, and it's two in the afternoon." I was astonished that he would say such a thing given the history of the Black Panthers and Malcolm X and the fact that he preached the Bible in a Harlem storefront. Incidentally, like many other accountants for smaller firms, I was also the human resources department; I fancied myself as a humane socialist in that capacity; I was definitely not a slave driver.

Some of my bosses were pretty smart when it came to knowing people and using them accordingly. They said I was "much more than a bookkeeper." They wanted me up front, conferring on strategies, hanging out in meetings, flying about the country troubleshooting and the like, at least until I lost my some front teeth and refused to replace them. But my accounting duties were best done when I was left alone in the back offices where I could concentrate on the books and analyze the numbers.

Sometimes I felt like a financial desert prophet. All too often I delivered the financials to the executives with dire predictions. Financial disaster was inevitable, I pronounced, unless certain steps were immediately taken to increase revenue and conserve resources; curb theft and curtail expenses; acquire loans and obtain investments; and the like. And live as if you are in poverty during prosperous times, I said, and you shall do well in bad times. Deficit spending was a mortal sin in my conservative black book of accrued balances. If a corporation could not employ resources so as to minimize expenses to its customers while paying labor decent wages and providing a fair return to investors and owners, I figured it ought to be dissolved instead of being allowed to run up bills everywhere.

As for my personal budget, which was puny indeed, my sole objective was to save up enough money to buy the leisure time to retire to libraries where I would naturally read and write books. All the while I sincerely believed that I would become one of the greatest writers the world would ever or never know. I successfully pretended to be a bookkeeper, accountant and corporate comptroller, but I was in reality a natural born creative thinker and literary artist at heart. I avoided getting stepped on by the lords of land and business. I saved up for years and years, and then one day I up and quit my job and took up writing.

One might say that I badly blundered, risking my life's savings on such a vain enterprise at my age, just as Social Security was going down the tubes because neoconservatives needed more wealth for themselves and their heirs. As a matter of fact, I thought I had made a terrible mistake at the time, but I insisted on persisting in my vanity against my will to survive. Lo and Behold, I was offered the accounting position of my dreams shortly thereafter - some say the Devil was afoot. By virtue of an incredible act of virtual suicide, I then turned down power aplenty along with two paid vacations annually to anywhere in the world; a substantial salary invisible to the IRS, exemption from foreign taxes by special dispensation of the prime minister; pilot's training and access to a small plane; and access to tax avoiders from all over the world. What especially alarmed me about the deal was all those goodies were to be had with a tourist visa and the naked promise of a prime minister. I headed west to pursue my ideal career, to be a bookworm instead of a glorified bookkeeper in a banana republic. After all, I told myself, I was conditioned to be a man of many words, not a numbers man. Moreover, according to an occupational preferences test I took, my preferences would be fulfilled as an author, professor, lawyer, bookstore manager, public relations director, or hairdresser. Crunching numbers was dead last on my preference list: you will find me with the artistic types at preferential cocktail parties.

I originally took up full charge bookkeeping in Hawaii simply because I was flat broke. Fate does not always cooperate with personal destiny. I did what I had to do to survive in paradise, lest I be kicked out of it by the lord of the land. I used my ten-key adding machine skills to add up and balance the night transcript at one of Roy Kelley's Surf hotels. That took me no more than six hours each evening, leaving me two hours to goof off. After I left that job, I liked to walk by late at night to see my replacement struggling to balance the transcript, sometimes having to work overtime to get the job done.

I took my cash savings and ventured to the Mainland with the idea of marrying a tourist I had met. I got cold feet and returned to Waikiki, checking into the hotel where I would be robbed that night, putting me onto the street with a quarter to my name the next morning. Jim and Mary Ann Sewell from New Zealand took me in two days later, Mary Ann, when she found out I was a crack ten-key adding machine operator, said I could make a decent living if I learned how to be a full charge bookkeeper, and she hired me to handle accounts payable at B&G Sightseeing, where she was controller. I rose rapidly from accounts payable to keeping the general ledger and cranking out financials and performing other duties associated with being a bookkeeper, accounting manager, and corporate controller.

Now here I am at the beginning of the end, millions of numbers and words later, writing my swan song at the edge of the very grave I dug for myself. I do not have faith in the Vanity of vanity, of rising from the dead to eternal life, but I do crave verbal immortality. After my years as a faithful button-pusher and key-banger on the ten-key adding machine, typewriter keys and computer keyboards in order to invest the proceeds in literature, I dread more than ever the idea that my beloved work might be discarded by society after I am gone. The Hindus say the body is just a coat to be discarded. My ideal body is my corpus, and the thought that it might be tossed aside after my physical body disintegrates disturbs me to no end. And that gives me further cause for hope; history is a series of mistakes we would avoid if we could. I might bloom late if that be my fate, and enlighten some small part of the world with brilliant essays and novellas.

Machines and Me

SOMEONE ONCE SAID that a thief is a capitalist without capital, but I was too square to steal the means of production: I occasionally worked the lathes, drill presses, punch presses, and grinders, but I did not stoop to steal a machine. Several bouts of unemployment along the random course of my youth had given me cause to take any kind of job I could get, so after washing dishes I landed in machine shops for a spell. I drilled countless holes and even turned out thousands upon thousands of left-handed screws besides right-handed ones; and, among other things, I put the wooden handles on tile knives and sharpened barrels and barrels of them on the grinder.

I shan't forget the poor man I worked with at a Minneapolis machine shop. He was overcome by fumes from the degreasing tank as he leaned over it to wash a basket of oily parts: he fell into the degreasing tank and drowned. As if that were not enough to ruin the day, I had ignorantly placed my liverwurst sandwich on the housing of a idle machine, where it grew so rancid from the heat after the machine was turned on and until noon that my stomach violently turned just after I gobbled down a big bite to comfort myself after the ambulance had left with drowned man's body. Several of us got drunk at the corner pub in our fallen comrade's honor. I am ashamed to say that we inadvertently sideswiped a few parked cars on the way home, but never mind. I stumbled into my girlfriend's apartment, collapsed on the floor and vomited up a pink solution of beer and sloe gin on her white rug before I passed out.

Although I did not know what I was doing, my girlfriend married me because I loved her and that is what girls do. Life was tough and bitter cold in The Cities, so we moved to Topeka, where I had family; as if that would do us any good, since I had ran away from that family years before because it was not good for me, and I hardly needed a daily reminder of my youthful indiscretions as a frustrated juvenile delinquent – mind you that I was basically a good boy who was wrongly accused of being bad, hence I took the suggestions in one way or the other and got even.

I understand that 'topeka' is a Native American term for "a good place to dig potatoes.' But it was especially difficult for a young paleface to get a job in Topeka; not to mention the impoverished Indians or the poor Mexicans who lived in tar paper shacks near the railroad tracks. I declined an offer to climb into fuel storage tanks, newly fabricated for filling stations, and to weld the seams together; or rather, I accepted the job but quit before I showed up. Instead, I took a job at a machine shop; its main customer was Goodyear. Two months later, the union steward got me fired on the pretext that I was incompetent. I had been unwittingly stamping out nearly twice the quota of parts on one of the punch presses, which had aroused the ire of the journeymen. Wherefore the shop steward gave me a task far beyond my competence as a barely experienced apprentice: to dismount a large motor from a huge upright lathe used to turn out tire molds, and mount it on a different type of machine. After I was fired, I resolved never to work at a machine shop again, and I swore I would stay away from rednecks who chew tobacco and have an unseemly habit of grabbing the crotches of their coveralls every ten minutes or so.

I found a night job cleaning the potato chip machine at Frito Lay. The chip machine was laid out along the length of the building to convey and process the potatoes dumped into the hopper at one end. The spuds were scrubbed; the stones dug up and shipped with them sank to the bottom; and then the washed potatoes were dropped into a rapidly spinning cuff; thanks to centrifugal force, they were sliced into chips by the razor sharp knives in its sleeve. The chips were conveyed by a series of paddles along a long cooker full of oil, from which they arose along an incline, dripping off much of the oil, under a huge salt shaker at the top of the incline, and then dropped onto a shaking table which rid them of excess salt and oil. Part of my job was to climb up to the salt shaker with 50 lb bags of salt and load it for the morning shift.

But for one other man, the fellow who ran the cheese-puff machine, I had the plant to myself at night. The puffs were made by forcing flour mixed with other ingredients through a hot collar with holes in it. Although he let me operate the machine during his breaks, and told me about the guy at the saloon who found a thumb in his potato chip bag, I did not like him very much, as he was a spitter and was wont to spit into the large cardboard boxes as they filled with puffs.

Cleaning the chip machine was not a bad job; I worked well without supervision. After washing the machine I spread lye on the concrete floor and hosed it down. I could literally hear the rot oozing from the crates late at night: somewhat rotten potatoes were cheaper and made good chips, with delicious brown rings in them. My job climaxed every morning when I started up the machine: I turned on the gas jets and leaned my upper body into the huge oven, using a burning broom as a match to fire it up so the oil would be heated for the early shift.

I lost the job when Pepsi took over; the main topic of conversation had been the virtue of buying stock before the buyout, but I had nothing to spare on my lowly pay. My wife was pregnant, and now I was out a job, strapped with car payments. I asked the bank to repossess and sell the car, a chrome-laden white Impala convertible with red interior. I was car crazy in those days, and had purchased it with a settlement my wife had received for a car accident. I suppose we were better off without it, as it was always breaking down: it broke down on its new owner just after he bought it at the auction, and sat alongside the highway for several weeks.

Things were not going very well in Topeka, to say the least, and we were reduced to eating mostly potatoes. Almost flat broke, I filled out an application for welfare. The lady from welfare visited us just as the car was being towed away. She was so rude and contemptuous that I ordered her out of the house and resolved that I would never accept welfare as long as I lived. I told my wife that I would rather steal food from grocery stores and rob banks than be a welfare recipient. Two hours later the police came to the door, arrested me for nonpayment of five one-dollar parking tickets, and threw me in the cooler with a bunch of drunks.

Fortunately for the future of my young family my father paid the tickets and the fine; I did not have the thirty dollars, and I would have had to serve thirty days in jail to work it off. As luck comes in streaks, I found a job the very next day, fabricating aluminum window frames for a company whose main customer, Holiday Inn, was expanding. Our pay included one silver dollar every week. It was good to have another job: I bought another car, a tornado hit the capitol building a block from our apartment, and President Kennedy was assassinated.

We see hollow aluminum framing everywhere we go, usually in store fronts. Truckloads of aluminum extrusions came in from Georgia. A journeyman cut them into the right lengths with a circular saw – one man cut his hand off on purpose. I drilled holes and riveted brackets onto the ends of the hollow aluminum lengths so they could be assembled in the field and glass installed in the frames. One day I forgot that my hand was inside the end of a length of aluminum extrusion as I was drilling a hole in it, so I drilled a hole clean through my hand. That hurt badly but did not do much damage as the drill slipped off the bone and glided through the muscles. On the way to the hospital I resolved that someday soon I would get away from laboring on dirty and dangerous machines, and return to the typewriters and adding machines I had had some small experience with earlier on.

OMG-D I might be Moses!

I *think I was an Egyptian scribe in a previous life.*

I MANAGED TO TRADE MY BLUE COLLAR for a white collar once and for all. My office career saved me from having to actually produce or sell things. I studied primers on management and discovered that managers are not supposed to actually do the dirty work but should get others to do it. Yet I was not fully committed to management given my inherited proletarian disposition. Mind you that my kind of proletariat had just learned to read and write; he likes to protest and does not plan on seizing the factories quite yet.

If only I had lived the life of the most middling bourgeois, steadily advancing to a middle management position while investing a portion of my income in a diversified portfolio, I would now be comfortably retired, free to write to my heart's content or to go sailing instead. Yes, I might have a boat in my driveway, or perchance, by virtue of the Dot.com mania, a modest yacht in the harbor. Even a career in the military and the right Fidelity funds would have made me a more substantial man today in terms of waistline and wealth.

But I really did not want anything, not even that yacht some men would die for. Indeed, I saw such a man and yacht shortly after I took up double-entry bookkeeping in Honolulu. The gentleman had apparently retired to live his golden years in Hawaii. He was heading his craft towards Honolulu's Ala Wai Yacht Harbor in heavy seas, and the waves heaved the vessel into the boulders alongside Magic Island. He jumped overboard between the boulders and his vessel and tried to push it off the rocks; each wave threatened to pin him against the rocks.

We kept yelling for him to climb out of there, offering him one end of a pole, but he persisted and was crushed by his beloved hulk. I did not admire his heroic effort at the time: I simply thought he was a foolish man, and observed a pair of large frigate birds circling overhead as if they were a sign of something or the other.

In retrospect that frustrated sailor has my deepest sympathy. I was indubitably a fool myself, perhaps even more foolish than he. Everyone must have something to live for besides life in itself; that is to say, they must have a way of living or living is for naught, and that way is of course limited to something or the other. That my thing is metaphysical and his thing was physical does not make me a better man than he nor any the wiser. Those of us who are so fond of the profound depth of our inner lives as we worship the vanities of our vanity should pause to consider the contents and reaches of the universe, in respect to which our inner profundity is exceedingly shallow or vapid.

Still, my favorite things are of the mind. I write therefore I exist, and I exist all the more when I write stories about myself, such as this one. I lived well below my means no matter how much I earned at a job, and for good reason: I wanted to buy time to write stories. Yes, I have perused and enjoyed the ocean-going literature, but I have never coveted a real yacht nor have I sailed let alone been on one. Suffice it to say that I wanted an ideal, a golden ark, if you please, that would carry soulful seeds for the implantation and evolution of my most grandiose dream – nothing less than the mental salvation of humankind, in which kind I mercifully included scribbling myself. I even wrote of writing myself to death to that altruistic end. Wherefore I did not cast my lot with the greedy bourgeoisie, whose mechanical institutions were efficiently and effectively grinding human beings to dust, leaving them to eat pig-ear sandwiches while their masters lived high off the hog – may Sacred Scripture forever forbid it with a pox on the swinish bourgeois if not an Armageddon!

Only bookworms can live on books alone. Today's books are poisoned for preservation, the caretakers caring not for the Worm in their urge for property. Unable to live on the pages I read and wrote, I stooped to keeping books of account to support my spiritual calling. Yes, I confess: I was a lowly bookkeeper for my miserable keep. I mean I counted other people's filthy lucre. Yet I was redeemed because I never really wanted their burdens. It simply was not my calling to grimace at a desk under florescent lights, as they habitually do in the infernal commercial quarry where they are crushed daily by the virtual rocks in their heads – Sisyphus never had it so badly in Hades. But whatever my calling is, an office job has been my lot.

Ironically, I have a knack for business, providing that I do not own it. I might have been Pharaoh's scribe in a previous life, rising in the ranks from superintendent of tomb construction to chief keeper of seals. If the legendary Moses actually lived in Egypt, he might have been an ancestor of mine. I might be him reincarnated, ordained to become the greatest lawgiver the world will ever know if not a bestselling author. Shall I memorize the Decalogue and grow a long beard? Oh, no, it is too difficult to remember ten things and perchance divine why the injunction against murder is sixth on the list when one is distracted by the wonders of this wide world of ours. Ah, who knows how I will turn out? That my beard turns gray is no doing of mine!

On My One-Sided Conversations With Women

MY ONE-SIDED CONVERSATIONS with women, none of whom is really interested in me enough to care if I were in a terrible accident, reminds me of this little poem written by my father. Bruce Campbell Walters and entitled 'Vagrant Wind,':

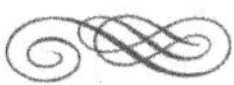

ALSO THIS PHENOMENON I note:
When I write letters whose recipients
after several intervals of several months
answer and do not discourse on items I have raised,
or speak to questions that I ask,
but each—uniquely poised at central point
of each one's world—relates to me she saw a cloud,
or comments on a vagrant wind along the grass where she resides."

IT IS NOT THAT I BLAME my female interlocutors for their exceeding self-interest or vanity; they would naturally accuse me of the same; but men know better when they try to get a word in edgewise on the phone.

What we have here is a phenomenon rooted in biology, first of all, then religious and political culture; religion is the worship of absolute power and politics is the distribution of that power, males getting the lion's share in the beginning. Females need protection and compete for it by making themselves as attractive as can be, thus putting the Cosmos in order, at least cosmetically, for they are often abused at home by their guardians.

Naturally females do not have a monopoly on vanity; all are not exceedingly vain. Men are becoming increasingly so, as conservatives say, with the "feminization" or "emasculation," call it "civilization,' if you please, of men, and the "masculinization" of women. That is why I think my father, who wanted to bring the hidden woman in man out, used the pronoun 'he" in his observation.

Why, just the other day, a man at the gym, a veteran sniper who claims to have killed over 200 men, women, and children in the Vietnam Police Action, and two more in his front yard after he got home, and then two more in prison, pointed out men with buttock-implants and beards at the gym, and said he would not kiss any one of them with mouth-to-mouth resuscitation if they collapsed because he is a real man.

Well, vanity falls along a continuum, and some people have more reason than another for being preoccupied with their egos in our individualistic culture. Now it is said that the vainest man in the world is the President of the United States, leaving one to wonder what American the Great has come to. Folks who are sick and tired of the war of all against all, with the vanities of this civilization, would love to have their egos absorbed by a Great Man with simple solutions.

Thankfully, great men could care less about someone like me; and neither does my best female friend, who likes to call me "Loser" for not having the things I worked hard to free myself from.

In fact, when a woman starts taking a personal interest in me, I panic, especially if she has a beard. I guess I am too self-interested, and maybe vain as well for exhibiting my opinion on this subject!

Loser

"LOSER!" YELLED THE MAN contemptuously at me as we passed in front of the bodega on Sixth Street.

I stopped in my tracks, turned and looked after him as he continued towards Meridian Avenue. He was darkly complexioned yet he had hurled the standard epithet at me without the usual Hispanic accent. I am, you see, one of the few 'gringos' living in my neighborhood, a foreigner in my own country.

"He's dingily dressed," I thought. "He looks like a loser himself."

Now there's a word for you, 'dingy,' derived from 'dung,' suitable to the ghetto at the butt end of Flamingo Park, once known as Seventh Heaven, the crack hood between Fifth and Seventh. The cops have been trying to clean it up lately.

"Millions of people would love to live here," said a cop who responded to a rape on the steps of the building behind mine awhile back.

I don't blame them after watching the evening news and seeing the Third World. My allegedly raped neighbor from Guatemala would later be arrested for lying to the police because she did not want her husband to know about her drunken tryst with two of his pals on the steps while he was slaving away in a South Beach kitchen. She had passed out. A neighbor thought she was dead and called the police, and her regular mate showed up.

"*Me violaron, me violaron*!" she cried when she saw him.

So I live in a loser neighborhood, relatively speaking, but why would a fellow loser be calling me a loser? I had not seen him previously. I am going on eighty-years old, so how could he know that I was the anchor man who dropped the baton at junior high school track meet, causing our relay team to lose the state championship?

"Loser, loser, loser!" chanted the kids in the stands. And since that day I was called "loser" by kids in the halls of Middle School. The coach's little talk about sportsmanship and respect was of no avail, for every American kid worth his salt was made to understand there are only two kinds of people in the black-and-white world: losers and winners. I went on to prove myself by dropping the football just before I got to the goal line, costing us the division championship: again I heard the chant, "Loser, loser, loser!"

Oh, I was a loser on the baseball field too, where I dropped the ball, allowing the winning run to score in the championship game. And, yes, on the basketball court too. The black underdogs were showing the world a thing or two: The white underclass players were getting themselves elbowed under the basketball net by 7-foot African Americans. The dominating movements would be celebrated by white kids doing the Watusi dance in the 70's.

I think my coach had contempt for me, condemning me as a loser despite his political correctness: Never again would I be in the in-group he shared World War II stories with. He often showed us "The Trophy," the mummified penis he said he cut off a dead Japanese soldier. Taking our cue from the bloody history we loved, we were eager to follow in the bloody footsteps of our forefathers when the inevitable police action in Vietnam rolled around. Death does not seem to be such a big deal when you are young. Much of a long life is wasted on cowardice and piling up shekels for nothing.

I was willing to kill Charlie, as the Viet Cong were called from the 'Victor-Charlie' phonetic for VC, not because I thirsted for blood, but because I could not find a job and wanted to feed my family. I signed up for the Navy because I figured I would have a better chance of survival if I worked on a ship. Here again I was fated to lose. I was arrested running across the street with a box of food I had stolen from a local grocery store. The recruiters could not help me. My father saved me. I had lived with him for four years after he retrieved me from a foster home where I, apparently born to lose, was placed when I lost my mother. I regret that I hated him sometimes. He worked wonders for me, I think because of his legal training, and I was not sentenced to prison, nor do I remember being on probation, for that matter.

By the way, I was not ashamed except that I got caught and that I was unable to get a job no matter how hard I tried. I knew that Plains Indians made an honorable living stealing. Their favorite name for the whites who stole their lands while preaching Christianity was 'liar."

I believe civilized people should have a right and duty to participate in social endeavors, and a right to humble housing and food and medical care for their families. Without that, they have a natural right to survive by any means. Today, many people at the apex of the social pyramid are successful thieves. In fact, I knew several highly regarded men and women back in the day, but I keep my trap shut although they look down on me.

My father did not condemn me for getting in that kind of trouble. He lived through the Great Depression. His mom had a job with the state, but the pay was so low that she served pet food to the family on occasion — wealthy families spend more money on pet food in fancy packages nowadays than poor families have available to feed their children. He had to borrow shoes for his high school graduation ceremony. He reenlisted during World War II because he said the Army was like having a mother and father, somewhere to sleep and plenty to eat. He worked in a shoe store after he was discharged, and then there was law school, the real estate business, the tragedy of my mother's death, abject poverty, decent pay as a member of the brotherhood of electrical workers, a disabling injury on the job, and living hell at home.

I endured hell. I ran away from home to Chicago's streets a week after my 13th miserable birthday. I contacted my father when I was sixteen because I needed his consent to marry at sixteen. I went back south. A child soon followed, and then another. I lost a temporary job cleaning a factory floor and painting its walls. I hocked my beloved accordion and stole an expensive level off a construction site to sell for food to feed my family. I returned to Chicago with my family, was arrested, and I finally agreed to be extradited although my attorney, paid for by my father, said he could delay justice indefinitely.

My father came through again; I shall never forget how furious the prosecutor was, yelling "He fought me like tiger!" after the judge freed me over a legal technicality. My father packed me in a car and rushed me to the state line. I returned to Chicago, where I had a railroad job and an apartment with my family. Born to lose, I soon lost my family because I did not heed my dad's advice, "Never let your wife work or she will get ideas and leave you." I wanted so badly to make a family that the loss utterly crushed me, and my father said he feared for my life\

I was a delinquent young man with some goodness in me, and like Moses, I was reforming, but it was too late as far as my wife was concerned, so off she went with the kids to further marriages. I tried to lose myself with a bottle of sleeping pills I downed downtown, but I lost my bid for peace and woke up with stomach pumped and tied to a hospital bed, where I was told my wife wished me dead. The doctor threatened to have me committed to a nuthouse. My dad was not there to save me.

I think my mother's spirit got me out of the hospital and other scrapes. I had lost her to the polio epidemic when I was eight-months old; she was twenty two. I heard about her from my dad; he kept writing poems to her, hoping to resurrect her somehow until he died, aged ninety, shortly after saying he was pleased to know what had been ailing him. I dubbed it the 'Orpheus Complex' because Orpheus recovered his wife from the Underworld; but the doctors at the VA diagnosed him as 'paranoid-schizophrenic.' The tough, veteran he-man was wearing dresses to reincarnate my mother, blaming his transvestitism, however, on his own mother's practice of dressing him like a girl when he was little in Pittsburgh, where his father tended bar, brewed beer, and whipped him when he found him in a dress.

Father was strange yet crazy intelligent. He was in one of the last cavalry units, and he loved horses. Steeped in romantic literature, his hero was Lawrence of Arabia, whom he considered to be a military genius. I knew my father, as I said, only briefly. I figured he was working a con, wreaking vengeance on society by behaving weirdly. After all, I was a weekend Hippie by that time, definitely a loser after smoking weed, dropping some acid and protesting against the war in Vietnam I had initially wanted to participate in.

I had gotten lost just in time when I ran away: My dear brother, sister, and their mom suffered worse than hell in their house of horrors, where my brother said our dear old dad crawled up and down the stairs like a snake, screaming in pain from his industrial injury. When he got back on his feet, he embarrassed my stepmother by showing up at her job dressed like a woman. And he liked to brag that his disguise was so perfect that he frequented ladies' rooms undetected. Mind you that he assured everyone that he was not gay and had never been with a man. His best friend was gendered-changed nun. He was furious many years later when I introduced him as my aunt.

I lost touch with him after I returned to Chicago for the last time. I did not want to be found. I moved on to New York, and then to Hawaii, where I lost another wife, dearer even than my first, one whom I still think I might get back with if she has not passed away to the Better Place. I went back to New York, where I struggled for several years, studied the performing arts, gained good day jobs, abandoned art on the verge of success, quit a great job, found a better one offshore but managed to lose it before I shipped out. I returned to Hawaii and spent my savings, went back to the Mainland to attend to my father for a while, and then on to Florida, where I had been before along with many other losers, and where I would one day receive my father's ashes in the mail.

I naturally blamed my father for the loss of everything I had gained in the Big Apple. I had made no effort to contact him over many years. I figured he was dead. Somehow he found my phone number and called me in New York out of the blue. The sound of his domineering voice dragged me back to hell on Earth. I ran away from fame and fortune in an effort to regain my long lost family.

Why, a prominent magazine had sent out photographers to take pictures of me in the dance studio at Carnegie Hall, and then a whole day shooting in Central Park, and another day at my little crib on the Upper West Side, an illegal sublet from a famous singer who had lost his voice to a paralytic neurosis. And a man named, Dennis, a headhunter, math genius and writer, had befriended me to secretly write a book about me, whom he perceived as a sort of Phoenix destined for greatness after arriving at Penn Station with five dollars and a little suitcase. He abandoned the project when I left, revealing the cause of our relationship, cursing me and saying he had given the book a new title, 'Loser,' before getting drunk and destroying the manuscript in a fury. I heard later that he had been struck and killed by a subway train when drunk, reminding me of how I had lost my best friend Billy when he jumped to his death from the Beacon Hotel on Broadway. That recalled how my two best friends in the Fifth Grade, twins, had hung themselves in their garage after their father, a Korean vet, hung himself there.

The readers I have not yet lost may think I must have been miserable indeed after such a string of losses, and they may wonder why I did not lose myself. Well, I was especially miserable about losing my first wife hence the suicide bid, which I lost, of course. Yes, I was miserable, yet I blamed myself for that. I sat down in the depths of despair in Central Park with my only friends, the trees, and a gun one day, and I asked if I wanted to be so miserable. The answer was No, but

I was afraid to lose my body so I educated myself to not feel miserable over the loss of things. One method I resorted to was to get rid of things and relationships before I lost them, and to take a loss on my stock on a dip just before it tripled.

I became a nihilist, worshiping Nothing, telling myself that Nothing is perfect. I still liked people and nice things, but I did not want to depend on them. I wanted only enough to subsist on. My only fear is to wind up dependent in a hospital room one day.

Women no longer take an interest in me. I have nothing to offer but words, of which I am overly generous, even knowing that my good advice, not to make the countless mistakes I made, will be wasted. Ladies looking for "a generous man" have called me "a loser." I don't mind if they do, for I consider myself a successful loser without them.

I am tempted here to recount a few more losses, but I shall not bore the audience that I have probably already lost. I mentioned that I was born to lose, but not to the extent of making "born to lose" a motto tattooed on my arm and murdering nurses. My kind is accursed enough. Many of us are like fireflies, our family insect, or flashes in the pan, brilliant lights, immediately dimmed and extinguished. Every other male in our branches may be predisposed to drug and alcohol addiction. The females are prone to exhaustion after accomplishing some slight reforms in their men.

My father warned me long ago: He said, ever so ominously, that we are like the seed that fell on rocky ground. I had no idea of what he alluded to until just recently, when I obtained a barely legible copy of my great-grandmother's journal of her ordeal in Pittsburgh, *The Seed That Fell On Rocky Ground*.

The seed that fell on rocky ground did not have much soil. It sprang up immediately in shallow soil. When the sun rose, it was scorched and withered away because it had no root.

Yet Sadie Walters accomplished a great deal for humankind in Pittsburgh before she had a heart attack while cleaning a floor. She wanted to go on a tour with her book and have it made into a new-fangled motion picture so her struggle would be a lesson for young people. That struggle is still our struggle, so I have resolved to execute her will before I lose my life, and that despite a friend who says I am a loser who never finishes anything. Another says my work has done many people a lot of good, so there is still hope.

On The Urge To Gratuitous Violence

I DON'T KNOW ABOUT YOU, but I felt like making a contribution to Gratuitous Violence when I got up this morning; that is, something in me would commit some violent act for no discernible reason.

Indeed, I cannot say that I was mad about anything in particular, say, angry at the authorities who are depriving people of the few liberties they have won over the past two centuries in order to save them from the coronavirus, destroying their livelihoods in the process so they can vent their anger over a Great Depression by engaging in mass murders worldwide to revive the economy.

No, my inexplicable urge to do something violent, like go out and behead someone at random or blow up the police station or smash Macy's windows had no motive that I wanted to know about. Something inside me wanted it kept secret. I understand that if the truth be told, this is quite normal.

My father told me during my juvenile delinquency that I have a Conflict With Authority. He had suffered from it himself. He reenlisted during the war. serving as an MP and drill sergeant before he got mad and was demoted for rebelling against authority. At least he was understanding enough not to smack me around when I acted up, I think because I reminded him of my mother, who died of polio before I was a year old and whom he promised to take care of me; he later truly said he should have left me with an orphanage. He was one of those old-school, domineering dads who scared the hell out of kids although he did not hit them, and he frightened the hell out of mothers and stepmothers who in turn took the abuse out on the kids, especially the boys. No thank you said I to myself and ran away to Chicago at age 13 never to return. I have been running away from the home I never had ever since, particularly when on the verge of success in whatever endeavor I chose to escape from the reality of how miserable I was.

In any event, I turned my anger at others against myself, meaning I am more suicidal than homicidal in the final analysis, yet I have indeed been loved enough to love myself hence curtail my violent tendency. I sublimated my propensity to violence by retreating to reading, eventually preoccupying myself with the arts of dance, drama, and writing. The last was my first and last resort, lately in the form of diatribes and rants against authority.

Are not the creative arts essentially rebellious, that is, existential rebellions against being? I think Nietzsche on the one hand and Camus on the other were right about that, don't you? "Live dangerously," said the former, and "Create dangerously," said the latter. "Only artists hate this slovenly life in borrowed manners and loosely fitting opinions and unveil the secret, everybody's bad conscience, the principle that every human being is a unique wonder," said Nietzsche. "To create today is to create dangerously," said Camus. "Any publication is an act, and that act exposes one to the passions of the age that forgives nothing."

Ambiguity therefore skepticism makes received authority easy dialectical game. My fellow critics generally leave me be as I have a reputation for "dangerous intelligence," as one said after remarking that I could have a great career as a novelist; his way of calling me a liar for disagreeing with him.

What my critics do not know is that I am more than tolerant: I am basically a kind man, a bum at the bottom of my being who smiles a lot, and, when outraged, a rooster who backs down, a cowardly lion in search of courage. I favor the underdog whom I most vehemently disfavored when he was top dog. I eschew the overwhelming celebration of violence overflowing gratuitously from the media toilets although I do enjoy a well done satire on the subject now and then. Most violence is unnecessary when called for, perchance to naturally advance the race.

Divided against myself, I abhor gratuitous violence most of all. Therefore I wrote an essay on the subject:

The Art Deco Man

THERE IS SOMETHING TO THE NOTION that the characteristics of a person's personality is determined by where he lives for long. For example, we notice a remarkable difference between a desert Arab and an Appalachian hillbilly.

I awoke this morning after many years in South Beach thinking that I am an Art Deco sandbar man. I do not have jutting eyebrows like some of the lowbrows around town, but my skull is streamlined, and there is something superficial and cheap about me that I would preserve at all costs. I like the sand and dislike change, and I rather abhor the Mainland. Indeed, the farther I am from the Mainland crowd nowadays the better. I wish we could wall off the southern end of Miami Beach.

I would return to Hawaii if only I could, to be buried there hence become a genuine *kama 'aina* or 'man of the land.' Better yet be fed to the shark god. Honolulu was admittedly crowded, especially Waikiki, when I lived there, but my personality was affected by the Aloha spirit when I was controller for a tour company. Many of our escorts had a portion of native Hawaiian blood back then. My favorite escort played the ukulele and got suspended for two days because two drunken girls on his tour brawled over him in his Maui hotel room.

Hawaii is part of me for sure. I met a *hapa haole* girl on Oahu, a most beautiful girl, always had a serious expression on her face, and moved to Big Island for several years. There were not so many people there. Life in Kona was like living on the moon, what with all the lava around and a few puffs of Kona Gold every day. I liked to cruise around the island, pass the cane trucks in my Mark IV.

I am still somewhat spaced out although I have just said no for decades. A man from Honolulu recognized me in South Beach and said, "Are you still here? What the hell are you doing here? This is a shit hole, a big rip off." Well, I do sorely miss Hawai`i and that girl a lot, but what can I do? I am stuck in South Beach afraid of change because I had too much of it. Maybe I would go back if that girl would have me. I suppose she has remarried by now.

I went up to Alaska from Hawaii because a friend of mine needed help with his business. Alaska also became part of my personality, the high, cold and lonely part that wears a long beard and plaid shirts, the man who still yearns for that island girl and likes to harken to Richard Strauss' *Eine Alpensinfonie* and Wagner's Siegfried's *Götterdämmerung*. An Inuit told me that a proper man would sandwich himself in between two hefty ones to warm himself up in his Igloo, so I had my picture taken between two native girls in a bowling alley during the Anchorage Fur Rendezvous Festival.

That is how I fell in love with my last true love, a girl from Nome. I gave her a knife with a Walrus penis handle as a token of my affection. She was a tiny woman yet was strangely like me except she preferred wealth and chose a wealthy lawyer over me. I do not blame her. I have always been disinterested in money, too distracted by words to devote myself to accumulating more than I need for subsistence. Alaska spaced me out in a different way than Hawaii due to its vastness, the sheer height of its sky, the fact that it had three-for-one happy hours. And the adults preferred Coke while the kids played guitars and partook of Matanuska Thunderfuck.

Geography does make a lasting difference even when you move away from one place to another like the nomads of yore. I was born in the Sun Valley, in Phoenix, and that is why I liked to bake my head in the Sun. Polio took my mom away when I was little, so that was quite a blow, and there were other factors that cultivated loneliness in me, namely, what they call child abuse nowadays.

After Arizona, I wound up in a foster home in Oklahoma, where I was a relatively happy boy. It put the Okie from Muskogee in me, and I shan't forget those long drives to the Ozarks in the Nash, Gene Vincent performing at the park, the triple features on Saturday, the brown leather jackets, chewing on tar peeled off hot roofs, Camels and Lucky Strikes, the girl next door, growing watermelons, and so on. Sadly, my foster brother and his girlfriend slammed into a freight train and were decapitated.

My father eventually retrieved me from Muskogee and hauled me off to Topeka ('a good place to dig potatoes') where black people were marching around singing 'We Shall Overcome.' Home life was out of an Alfred Hitchcock movie. I rebelled, started drinking at 11, and hung out mostly with Mexican boys and a black family that lived downtown and liked to mix their whiskey in orange juice. I managed to wiggle away from the pervert who cruised around in a pickup truck. We moved to Lawrence by the great university. I still have a bit of the Jayhawk in me, and I have a corny sense of humor.

I could not stand home anymore, so I ran away to Chicago a week after my thirteenth birthday. It was tough on the streets although I did not have enough experience to know how bad it really was. I had watched The Untouchables as a kid, so I had an idea of how to behave. You had to be tough or at least act tough to survive the hoodlums not to mention freezing weather. One positive was the many runaway girls.

So I have some of that Tough Guy in me still, although I do not bite after I bark. Just the other day I had a run-in with a South Beach Tow truck driver over who had the right of way at an intersection, him, or a pedestrian in the crosswalk, namely me: He said he was amazed that a man my age would threaten to pull him out of the truck and beat the living hell out of him.

You see, I was born in the Year of the Cock. A rooster can be scary yet will back down rather than fight. I learned that in Kansas. I frightened an assailant so badly one time in Honolulu just by yelling at him and waving my hands that he fell over a chair and banged his head on a table. A soldier present who had not seen the whole thing accused me of picking on the guy, who had at least fifty pounds on me. After that, the local fellow always looked out for me.

What saved me from death or a life in prison in Chicago was the Midwestern work ethic I had picked up, even more solid proof of geographical determinism. Of course praying to my mother in Heaven helped as well. The city slickers taught me how to lie convincingly about my age and education, so I wound up with good jobs since people did not check credentials so carefully, or, by the time I was found out, I had made myself practically indispensable.

I met a wonderful girl from Minnesota. I moved to Minneapolis, and we married in Tracy. We moved to Kansas, then to Chicago. I was absolutely crazy about her. My previous family experience and training as a punk and juvenile delinquent so-called was dysfunctional. Of course the marriage failed; she was lucky, I suppose. Nevertheless, the consequences in terms of progeny are what my dad called "The Beautiful People up North."

I briefly resided in New Orleans' French Quarter before that marriage. I recall Oswald was there at the time. I practiced my Southern Accent and drinking Southern Comfort. I came down with malaria of all things. A student from Asia saved me, and put me on a bus back to Minneapolis. I still have New Orleans in me somewhere. Louis Armstrong was big. I liked that jazz better than the Kansas City jazz. I noticed plenty of people leaving the Quarter in body bags. The girls were pleasing for sure. I was introduced to the crabs, and my friend Jeff, whom I had hitchhiked to New Orleans with, got the clap and yellow jaundice, went gay and become a nightclub singer when he got out of Charity Hospital.

I lived in New York City three times. I went over from Chicago the first time, and it was wonderful because the drinking age was 18 back then whereas it was 21 for men and 19 for women in Chicago. I accumulated a good work history there. My main interest was literature and the performing arts. Dance was my big thing, something a Buddhist monk told me was for mentally ill people. I sang and acted relatively well. If it were not for my love of the written word, I probably would be a professional performer.

The concrete canyons, the crowds, the subways, the neighborhoods, the theaters, the bookstores, the bars, and the bridges of the New York all took a toll on me. An old friend of mine, a psychologist there, said I was a "therapeutic person" when I arrived the last time, from Hawai`i. I managed to become a "New York jerk" in short order. Why, a soldier at the Dallas airport said he knew I was from New York by watching how I boarded the airplane to Honolulu. I did not mind being called a New York jerk. I happen to like New York jerks to this very day. Once a New Yorker, always a New Yorker, even if you leave forever.

So yes, environmental determinism exists. I am, on the one hand, a monstrous hodgepodge of environmental influences slapped together at random. On the other hand, my personality is not absolutely random if nature has a big hand in determining nurture. My nature was once to wonder what I am, who I am, what or who made me, and why I am here if there is a why. Please do not tell anyone, but I do not think "I" exist. I gave up thinking about my "self," and I wondered instead about other metaphysical subjects.

A wonderer is a wanderer. I have wandered into a corner in South Beach. Nobody loves me because I do not have anything for them but words. I am an "old man" who has always thought, even at the age of five, when I first said it when my age was pronounced to me, that I am a million years old.

I no longer wander physically. I still wonder. It is a habit I have acquired, or maybe it is my nature. The end is nigh. I avoid it by thinking about something else, it matters not what.

I need a vacation at the very least. The natural and artificial environment is lovely in South Beach, but I am bored with Art Deco. Maybe a great deal of it should be demolished. I have been here too long.

Perhaps someone will see me an airport somewhere and say, "Hey, I recognize you, you're the Art Deco man!"

I Confess To Being An Alien

THEY SAY YOU CAN'T GO HOME AGAIN. I would try to go home if I could, but I have no recollection of ever being at home.

All I remember, and vaguely at that, of the beginning of my sojourn on earth, is that the mother ship, called Zero Base, was forced to land on this planet, and then there was a blinding light, and there I was, a human being.

My gracious host on Earth, my mother, Charlotte, died a few months later. I remember feeling unwanted in my grandmother's home, and then being left at a foster home, where I was treated well enough to dream of being back there for many years, but I was taken away unexpectedly by my father, who had remarried, to another state, where I heard my stepmother, on the night I arrived, screaming at him to get rid of me. Since then she did everything to convince him and me that I was a bad boy. She liked to beat me occasionally, to the extent that my father came home to find me knocked out on the floor.

So I was sent far away to military school for a year, much to my relief. Upon my return, my father informed me he could no longer afford military school, much to my dismay. He went off to work one day, and my stepmother, angered that he had bought me football shoes instead of a dress for her, fixed me breakfast, and, no sooner than I had sat down, she started hitting me on the back of the head with something, so I jumped up and left for good, less than two weeks after my thirteenth birthday. She found Christ and all was forgiven.

It was cold outside. I had no coat. I hitchhiked to Chicago. The fellow who gave me a ride in a car he had stolen to transport illegal fireworks for New Year's celebrations gave me a quarter for the elevated, and I wound up downtown, in the Loop.

This is not an 'Oh, woe is me' story, but is simply offered as evidence that once an alien always an alien. Yeah, it was rough going, but what does an alienated kid really know? I had a few things going for me. I was relatively intelligent. I had read The Three Musketeers, the Wizard of Oz, had seen Blackboard Jungle at the movie house, and had watched the Untouchables on TV. I was six-feet tall, and I could drink beer until I passed out.

Many of my runaway colleagues wound up in morgues and prisons. I may be the only one still alive. I wanted to work, not rob and kill people, burglarize homes and shoot heroin, pimp prostitutes and so on. Most of all, I wanted a home, and I tried my damnedest to have one. I would look into the windows at families and wish I had a family. I suppose bad training is no excuse for my failure to realize my dream, which resembled the Ozzie and Harriet show. The failure is not absolute, fortunately, for there have been successful consequences despite my shortcomings.

There was no Course in Happy Homemaking for me. My destiny is homelessness. By that I do not mean I have no shelter, that I am houseless. I mean I have never felt at home on this Earth, and it seems impossible for me to be at home. I am an alien. I often feel like I am hovering in a flying saucer, and do not dare to land. Aliens are unloved. I have done my fair share of loving, yet my love is flawed by alienation. Earthlings do not love me. It is too late. Nobody is going to adopt me as I used to wish. I have nothing to offer but stories.

No, I am not miserable except when I think long about what Buddha said about everyone suffering, and I perceive the fear behind the smiles. One thing I have learned is how to be content alone, and not to hate people. Why suffer needlessly? I cannot help liking even bad people to the extent I am human.

I used to retreat into a corner of a room and read to avoid Hell when I was a kid. Books were my best friends. My heroes were the authors who created the people and circumstances in them. Authors were gods for me. I identified with them, especially the ones who rode the rails in leather jackets and stole typewriters to write with.

I ran away from things, got into the world, lived in several cities, and threw away success several times when on its verge, and then I retreated into a smaller and smaller corner, a studio near the beach.

I shall not cry poor. I could be rich. I've helped people become rich, but that is not for me, because, you see, I am an alien to the things of this world. The first thing I want to do with a nice thing is give it away. Furthermore, much of what we call poverty is a cultural artifact: I live below the so-called poverty line. A cop responding to criminal activity in my building said millions of people would die to live like me, and she was correct although I do not want to be stabbed to death by the man who stabbed his wife seventeen times in the building next door while his friend watched and is wanted for two murders in Guatemala.

Now that I am approaching The End, I have an urge to run away again, at least to take a vacation from my alienation. I have lived most of my intellectual life in Europe although I have not set foot there. France is one of my favorite countries. I entertained the notion of vacationing there. Now I hear that I would be alienated there as an American because "American liberalism has ruined France."

Well, then, since I apparently suffer from what the French call dépaysement, I might take a French vacation, I could, as they say, "go to Tataouine." Or maybe I could go to Timbuktu. Since those places actually exist, I might just read Samuel Butler's Erewhon, or write my own book about Nowhere. After all, I am an alien if not a cosmopolitan everywhere I go, and, everywhere I go, there I am, so why go anywhere at all when I cannot get away from myself?

Still I would to see France. I have pleasantly dreamed of riding a train there. That was before the strikes. Maybe people there would like me if they knew I am not merely an American, that I am an alien.

Don't Quit Your Railroad Job

I WAS A MEMBER OF THE BROTHERHOOD of Railway Clerks when I was a young man in Chicago. I worked in the Freight Claims Department of the Legal Division of the Chicago, Milwaukee, St. Paul and Pacific Railroad, otherwise known as the Milwaukee Road, from July 1966 to June 1968.

Our main lunch topic was the number of years until retirement and how much was vested in one's retirement fund. Several years after I left the Road, a co-worker sent me a detailed letter on that very subject. And to this day I prize my letter of recommendation:

"Enclosed is copy of letter of recommendation you had misplaced. Good to hear from you and particularly your choice of residence. Hawaii would seem to be a great deal better choice than either Chicago or New York. We who are 'confined' to our railroad careers would have little to do in Hawaii. Let us hear from you further." L.E. Ruger, Assistant General Manager Freight Adjustment, June 25, 1975

"Mr. D.A. Walters has been employed in my office for two (2) years. He has proven to be a conscientious and capable employee and has good aptitude for learning and effecting office procedure. His employment covered various positions which developed into his being one of our claims investigating staff." Ken French, General Freight Claim Agent, July 16. 1968

I started at the bottom of the totem pole, in the mail room as the mail clerk. Then the file clerk quit so I got his job. I made a big impression on the office aristocracy—the Senior Adjusters and the Chief Clerk—when I came up with a better way of organizing the current claim files: taking them off their edges and stacking them flat in cubicles. Soon after that I was moved to my own desk in the main room, where I manually added long columns of figures on freight claims. We did not have adding machines. My job was to add them from the bottom up after the guy on the right added them from the top down, and we traded places every week.

I gradually climbed the career ladder and become a junior freight claims adjuster. The pay was so low I barely remember it. The pay scale for all workers was posted on the wall by the water cooler. My pay was enough to pay rent and to buy food with, plus a few bucks for a movie or ball game. Married people got bonuses for having babies.

I goofed up badly when I was working as a file clerk, but I was not fired. A fellow clerk and I snuck out of the building to a Cubs game a few blocks away. Unfortunately, the Chief Clerk saw us on TV. There we were, in the stands, cheering Ron Santo's home run and drinking beer when we should have been filing claim folders in the basement archives.

At a quarter to five every day, a steward came around with a cart of hot towels. We ritually wiped our faces and hands. Then all eyes were on the second hand of the large clock up front. The Chief Clerk donned his hat and abandoned ship, at one minute to five. Then the buzzer buzzed loudly, and off we went. Some went down the front elevator; the younger ones ran down the back stairs. To this very day, I still dream of running down the five flights of stairs. I also dream of the "Boston coffee" I liked to drink at the diner across the street.

The management was very considerate. For example, we were ordered to go home early on the days the blacks were rioting, and we were paid for that time off.

I loved working for the Milwaukee Road, so much so that I trudged to work during the big blizzard while Mayor Daly's cops were shooting at looters to kill. The office was closed when I got there, two hours after

I had started out. Boy, was I ever a dumb kid with a "Midwestern work ethic."

The Milwaukee Road was more than fair with me. I should have stuck around. Maybe I would be drawing that pension we talked about, instead of facing death on a park bench and writing articles at the public library.

Maybe this will be a lesson to fools like me. Don't quit your railroad job. I knew better, but I acted unwisely anyway. On the other hand, I might have done the right thing. The Milwaukee Road went bankrupt. I don't know what happened to the pension money, and that is the main thing.

My Early Inheritance

I DON'T CARE MUCH FOR THE BESTSELLING things and striking events of our times, but I do enjoy old books and the symbolic activities presented therein. I inherited my love for literature and a high tolerance for long lectures from my father at a very young age. Thanks to him, wonderful stories and academic discourses are my favorite things.

My father gave up journalism and became a dedicated 'Made in the USA' union man with the IBEW after the Great Depression and war. I disliked stripping the copper wire he brought home for extra cash, and I certainly did not want to become an electrician like him, but his love for the written word rubbed off on me. Wherefore I fancied myself as a proletarian writer at first, ever willing like Nelsen Algren to ride the rails to get a realistic gutter story if need be; Algren was so dedicated to his calling that he stole a typewriter and shipped it to Chicago before hopping a freight train back north; apprehended in transit, he did his jail time conjuring up the likes of Walk On The Wild Side.

Although I knew my dad for a very short period of time before I ran away from home for good, I was somewhat influenced by his delusions of grandeur and persecution, wherefore I am occasionally amazed by the grandeur of my own insignificance, as if I were at once both god and worm, and I don't mind saying so at considerable length. His family was impoverished by the Great Depression. He joined the Army, an institution that was, he claimed, "a refuge for outcasts and riffraff, and was just like having a father and a mother in those days, when a man didn't have any way of making a living." He was a cavalry and artillery man during the war, and a student of journalism, real estate, and the law thereafter. He met my mother towards the end of the war. After her death at age 21, he married another woman, and then another – in the interims I was a foster child.

My father was forced to take up a hard-hat trade to survive. An electrician by trade, he was a pipe-bending poet who wired, among other facilities, the Midwestern missile bases. He was an alienated union man in the good old days when long hours bending electrical pipe instead of the law could make one as much money as a lawyer – mostly immigrants want the construction jobs nowadays, and they fare slightly better than dishwashers. He carried a red-plastic-covered copy of The Sayings of Chairman Mao in his back pocket for some time. He also had a big wad of money close at hand, and hid quite a bit more between the pages of books. Moreover, he stashed gold contraband in the walls, so much that he forgot where he put it all –somebody is going to be pleasantly surprised when they tear down that place down.

His stash, he said, was for his escape from his circumstances. I assumed that included me, and most of all my stepmother, who hated me, so I wanted to escape before he did. He used to disappear until the wee hours of the morning, but he didn't a run for it until I was long gone, and he was virtually run out of town. A responsible family man, he just had to stay put through hell and high water. He liked to tell the story about the man who longed for many years to leave town, then went to the train station one day and died of a heart attack just as the train pulled in – sometimes people who enjoy suffering really do not want their ideals to be fully realized.

Now my dad, like me, was already balding in his teens. He was fond of saying that he had two personalities: hat on, hat off. But that was not all: he was also cross-dressing. Who would have known? He was a stern, tough-looking construction worker, a champion boxer in the Army, gung ho to go to the front line. He did not hesitate to knock a man out cold on Main Street one day, nor did he hesitate to shoot the neighbor's barking dog in the middle of night, after repeatedly warning its owner to shut it up – he said dogs should be canned and sent to feed poor Asians.

Hard as my father worked to support his last family and to make sure his wife never had to work and thus meet the competition, and as tough as he appeared to be, he was a sentimental romantic who cried over silly poems. Maybe that was because his mother dressed him up as a girl when he was a child; his bartending father came home and beat him for the confusion. Today he is a hapless Romantic who suffers from the Orpheus Complex: sixty years after her death, he still edits his poems to my mother, as if that would retrieve her from Death. At one point in his cross-dressing career, he took her name as his own. He said he was my surrogate mother for a short period after her death, and that he became convinced that the dresses his mother had clothed him as a child accorded with the real woman within.

Some time after he turned 85, he gave away his jewelry, bought two pairs of trousers, made washrags out of his fine dresses, and moved into a senior citizen's apartment on the grounds of a historic, gold-domed Catholic church. Keeping up the role of a woman was just too much for him at his age, he said. But he still looked a bit like a little old lady – it annoys him when complete strangers call him sweetie and dearie. Well versed in scripture, he refers to a messiah. One day, as he watched old folks creep from his apartment building into the side door of the church for Mass, he claimed that given the dissatisfactions of human nature, there is always a better place than our current residence, no matter where we are at the moment, and that the last resting place is what funereal preachers call the Better Place. His current flame is a lesbian nun, or rather a trans-sexual nun who says she is a lesbian bride of Christ.

There is some truth in the maxim: Like father like son. I am not inclined to wear dresses or to go overboard with my illusion into delusion. I have almost managed to rid my self of the romantic pathos.

But my father and I share our love for literature – it is our favorite escape from the brutal reality of realists who are subject to the illusions of realism. Today we identify a man with what he does to make a living, and not with the essence of his life. My father was a poet who happened to be an electrician. Some make good their escape and that is their living. Perhaps I shall differ from him in that respect. We shall see.

I Shan't Forget The Holocaust

NE OBLIVISCARIS, Never Forget, is the motto of my Campbell clan, the Clan of the Wild Boar. I shan't forget the Holocaust films of corpse-filled trenches they showed us kids at grammar school. Come to speak of it, my school chums and I were persecuted often enough. We were thrown up against the wall and had our ears boxed red for good measure, or we were ordered to the principal's office and smacked with a paddle with a hole in it when we were very bad. Jim Norton, my Mormon friend who wound up married to two women at the same time, got the worst of it; I'll never forget how he buried his head in his hands at his desk while the teacher thrashed him with a pointer stick.

We deserved every bit of it and more. Maybe corporeal punishment should be restored to private homes and public schools with a vengeance, considering how good we turned out as a consequence – Martin Luther was beaten several times a day everywhere he went, which got us our fine Protestant religion. Our crimes against humanity at grammar school were serious enough for our age. I got six resounding whacks for poking Anne Chandler in the wrong place while she was hanging upside down in the jungle gym. I made it up to her later, and kissed her in the alley on the way home. And Jim and I and Clifford Taylor, the only black boy in the school, peed in the finger-paint pots during recess, just before the finger-painting session; we could not help laughing our heads off as our peers smeared the paint. The teacher made a pointed inquiry: Clifford confessed, and we were roundly thrashed. But that was not the worst infraction at school: the janitor at our school was very mean to kids, as if he hated them for their opportunities; every morning he shined the old school bell mounted on a concrete pedestal at the entrance, so we defecated on it one night.

Not that I was all bad. One teacher knew that wayward boys need certain responsibilities besides taking out the trash at home, so he had me get the kindergartners lined up and march them around the block for exercise. I also was frequently assigned to walk one slightly retarded boy home when he got to smelling badly because he pooped his pants. And I was favored by my sixth grade teacher because when it came to reading and writing I was first in the class – I wrote my first brilliant story in sixth grade, about diving deeply into the water and finding a device that would save humankind. Yes, I liked reading and writing very much. I remember the little comic strips that came with Bazooka bubble gum. As for arithmetic, the multiplication tables were a pain to learn but I did my duty.

Of course sex was the most important subject in the fifth and sixth grades. I already knew something about the subject; my foster brother in Oklahoma got me started with the little girl next door when I was eight years old; consequently, and despite my grandmother's prohibition against touching it when going to the bathroom, I did not think there was anything dirty about sex at all provided it was between members of the opposite sex.

Anyhow, we learned to dance the Hop and the Stroll in grammar school. Furthermore, a voluptuous farmer's daughter with large breasts and broad hips was impregnated and married off to a third cousin. We were shown films on venereal disease, and one film discussed the health benefits of circumcision. Even more interesting, considering that some of us had just started smoking, was the film on reefer madness; we did not know what marijuana was until we saw that film, and then we wanted to try it. Yes, I remember those films very well. Ever so often the film would break and go flap, flap, flap, so we would have to wait and occupy ourselves with chitchat, or use our hands to make silhouettes on the white screen, until the teacher got it spliced and up and running again.

After we saw the film on the Holocaust, someone asked about communists; he said his dad had claimed that it was "better to be dead than Red." The teacher said communists were "Jewish intellectuals." We learned a good deal more about communism from a F.B.I. propaganda pamphlet in the library, and more than one boy decided to be a communist after reading it. The propaganda was confusing to me, for the teacher had told us that Jews were always counting money and hoarding it, so how could they be communists if communists wanted to take private property away?

Some of us grammar school boys were not only smoking but boozing before we went on to junior high school. Unfortunately for our local Episcopalian church, we walked the alleys to school and back: we found a crate of booze in someone's garage, got drunk regularly, and almost burned the church down one evening. We had slipped out of the Boy Scout meeting to buy Cokes from the machine in the hall, to mix the booze with, of course. We went upstairs to party and were soon in a drunken stupor. We played with matches and wantonly smoked cigarettes. The fire that destroyed part of the roof after we left the premises was unintended, its source being a smoldering cigarette. One otherwise nice boy, a Christian kid who thought he was Jewish because they were reading the Old Testament a lot in his Sunday School, had taken a dump by the organ; that evidence was dwelled on at length by the police department's psychologist. Pressed to confession, the imaginative anal expulsive boy claimed that the church was the burning bush from whence comes the voice of the Lord. He was suspected therefore of arson; he took the suggestion to heart and eventually became a church arsonist – he lost his life several years later, in a fire he had set in St. Louis.

The empty pint bottles left at the scene of our youthful indiscretion convinced the authorities that we were alcoholic juvenile delinquents.

We were consigned to four weeks confinement in a juvenile detention center, where we would hopefully be rehabilitated. We were allowed to smoke two Pall Mall's at the dinner table every evening. Ironically, I was released a week later on account of my heroism under fire. An unruly girl had set her mattress afire and the fire spread to two rooms. The husband and wife who ran the place were across the street, at the saloon. By the time the firemen arrived, I had already put out the fire with fire extinguishers. I was called a hero on the front page; my name was not mentioned because of my young age, much to my chagrin.

Notwithstanding the foregoing, I believed I was a good boy. I did not know why my pals and I became alley cats. Each set of parents blamed our leather-jacketed, duck-tailed waywardness on "keeping bad company," as if they and their kids were really better than the others. Mind you that we were by no means as mean as the Chicago and New York juvenile gangs we liked to read about in the books our parents took away from us, and in the movies they did not want us to see – so we snuck in the side entrance. In fact I was regularly accused of doing things I had not done, like stealing another kid's skivvies at the swimming pool, which sometimes gave me the notion to commit the deed I was accused of or even worse, out of spite for my accuser. I had sufficient reason to believe I was being persecuted not only by the authorities at school but by homely authority as well. Indeed, my father told me I was cursed with what he called "a conflict with authority." I remember his frequent references to his own persecution, by "the low-browed people," presumably the authorities who were in charge of small towns. After seeing the film about the Holocaust, I imagined my kind would eventually be gassed and thrown into pits.

My Reconciliation of Accounts

IT HAS BEEN SAID WE SHOULD BE CAREFUL lest what we wish for comes true. Well, I wished for a million of dollars on at least a thousand days, and I have no regrets since I am at least a billion in the hole today. Yet I have not abandoned my faith in the power of wishful thinking. I would not be altogether surprised if a few millions fell into my lap any day now.

I accept the fact that my destiny is not what I might wish it to be but is simply what it is. It is finally dawning on me that I was right all along: I was fated to be a bookkeeping author because that is what I am. It was no accident that the world afforded me the opportunity to pursue the art of writing for so long during this life of mine. I owe the world a better account of that life. Whatever I might be, I am an account payable. Only when my debt to society is paid with interest shall I feel reconciled with the world and be able to depart with the slate wiped clean.

"If you have always been an author," the reader might ask, "how do you explain all those years keeping books for businesses instead of writing books for readers? There is quite a difference between writing books and keep books of account."

I can explain, for that is part of what I do, explain things. I have managed to reconcile the two occupations according to the generally accepted principle of evolutionary accounting. You see, there was really no conflict between the occupations, for the writing of accounts had its origin in the keeping of accounts. Writing was simply a bookkeeping tool for many centuries before scribes started writing down their thoughts and became Egyptian literati, Jewish rabbis, Chinese scholars, Greek and Roman intellectuals, Byzantine kritoi and sekritoi, and the like- practical-minded, barbarian Anglo-Saxons are the late bloomers of the intellectual world. As long as scribes were comfortably ensconced in bureaucracies of stable countries, they naturally sided with the ruling class, whose treasure they accounted for and whose workforce they supervised.

The accounting profession became an avenue for commoners to move up in the world and to at least count the fabulous fortunes they did not own. And when the supply of intellectual workers exceeded demand during troubled times, they were thrown out of work or did not get their usual share of the treasure, intellectuals turned to the masses for employment as prophets, sages, and teachers. Literacy increases the ability of revolutionaries to communicate grievances and diffuse dissension, to bemoan the loss of golden eggs and advocate their reclamation or a cultivation of a new paradise. We see literature arise during troubled times: in Egypt with the breakdown of the Old Kingdom around 3,000 B.C.E.; in Sumer after the fall of the Third Dynasty of Ur about 2,000 B.C.E.; in Greece at the decline of the Mycenaean Age; in China during the Warring Period around 600 B.C.E.

Unemployed intellectuals have rightfully been feared and hated by barbarian-minded arch-conservatives throughout history. We are fortunate that so many intellectuals have been retiring types instead of activists with dictatorial aspirations. Mo Ti, a militarist who preached a doctrine of loving people afar as a practical policy of self-defense, remarked that the ruling classes of Chi and Chu "lost their empire and their lives because they would not employ their scholars." We should be careful with the knife lest we cut off too much fat from our seemingly absurd, gigantic make-work bureaucracies, particularly those that thrive on complex codes and modes for conflict resolution.

The experiences of the Hebrews in Egypt and Israelites in Babylonia, and the development of writing in general gave me cause to conclude that my bookkeeping experience was not wasted and that it may result in bestselling books. Verbal language, after all, evolved from counting or the mathematical recording of accounts; *cuento* followed *cuenta*. The earliest writing constituted accounting records. Primitive people could hardly count beyond three. The concept of number was a great leap forward in abstract thinking; for instance, that a man who had 3 goats, 1 pig, and 1 horse had, in sum, 5 animals, was bound to lead further, to broader written generalizations. The Hebrews wrote some of the earliest history books. One reason Hebrews, Israelites, and Jews were counted as an ambitious, land-grabbing, greedy lot is the fact that they accounted for their economic and other social exchanges early on in writing. We find a great deal of politics in the ancient texts; politics of course appertains to the distribution of power, one form of which is relative material wealth, the number of things a person has. Given the intense struggle for survival in those days, the ancient texts are naturally filled with matters of economic concern.

Wherefore there must not be any fundamental difference between the bookkeeping and book writing occupations. A bookkeeper may quite naturally become a writer of distinction, and, for that matter, a dancer and king. The lowly worm evolves into a godly authority. My underlying aspiration to be an author may have been my saving grace all along, and not the sponsor of the awful fate that seemingly impends at this juncture. In truth, I may be on the verge of the greatest breakthrough of my life, thanks to the fact that I quit that high-paying part-time account job I had in order to study and write full time. As if against my will, I was moved to invest my life's savings in speculation. Somehow I knew I had to make a complete break of it, no matter how financially painful that might be. Chinese historian Ssu Ma suffered involuntary castration in order to complete his histories. For once in my life I wanted to bring the drama to a fitting end instead of stopping short of the wings.

My account however remains payable. I danced full circle around the stage, and have taken another part-time accounting job, at half the pay, in order to write my swan song. I could have done all this ten years ago and in a comfortable lifestyle if I had kept the job I quit, but I did not know that at the time. The risk is much greater now, but the confusion less, for I have reconciled the old conflict in integrity - the integration of keeping business accounts and giving accounts of things real and imaginary.

I Was A Frustrated Newspaper Columnist

A PRIME MINISTER OF IMPERIAL CHINA started his career on the bottom rung of the ladder to success, cleaning the public outhouse. He observed the behavior of the rats – the fattest ones dared to make their way to the granary nearby, while the lean ones stayed put. He followed the fat rats' lead, improved his circumstances, and eventually made his way to the top.

"Why wait?" I asked myself shortly after I blew into Miami on the heels of Hurricane Jeanne in 2004, nearly flat broke and with no intention of taking up bookkeeping again to make a living. No, I was no longer a bookkeeper: I no longer kept accounts: I gave them. "Why not start at the top instead of the bottom? Why not land a column at top publication in town, The Miami Herald? I'll hit up the top man there for a column," I resolved to my alter ego, "and be the outstanding columnist that I am! Theodore Dreiser could barely finish a sentence when he pestered an editor into hiring him. Why not follow his lead? With my talent and skills, how can I not succeed?"

I whipped off an email to Tom Fiedler, the Herald's executive editor, purportedly one of the most reputable people in the newspaper business. I asked him to take a look at my work and to give me the break I deserved. I could obviously write up a storm about all sorts of things, the very activity that kept editors employed. I said I was well aware of the steps one is supposed to climb nowadays to become a newspaper columnist, but I felt obliged to skip them because I was a late bloomer who had insufficient time for the process. Besides, the steps were too slippery with decades of bullshit. Most importantly, I was already able to write the best column around – my work speaks for itself. Therefore I wanted him, one of the most admired editors in town if not this great nation of ours, to take me on at the Herald, so that I could enhance its prestige.

Mr. Fiedler responded at once – he did not bother to read the samples of the work I had attached to my email. Of course I was delighted that he responded at all, for few esteemed executive editors deign to personally answer email from nobodies in want of a work – perhaps my verbal kowtowing favorably impressed him. He said he admired my determination, and would not bother to parrot those who already have a high perch and are therefore wont to talk about the necessary rungs to climb before reaching a slot as a columnist at a major newspaper like his. Instead, he informed me, in his words, that a complex calculus comes into play in choosing columnists for the newspaper, a calculation that goes beyond the ability to write well; to wit: market need, experience, reputation, credibility in a subject, demographic profile – race, gender and ethnicity. He said some excellent writers simply never get a column because they're in the unfortunate position of not being the right something-or-other to suit the paper's needs at the time when an opening occurs. In other words, he said, he could not alleviate my frustration, although he wishes me the best.

Would I take a polite "no" for an answer? Hell no, I would not! An honest panhandler would surely curse anyone who turned him down, and a serious candidate for a newspaper column would put up an honest fight for the job. I confess that I resent rejection so much that I thrive on it, doing everything in my power to elevate my high opinion of myself over the opinions of those who fail to subserve mine. Of course my supererogation gives them further cause to reject me with nary a word in response for fear that, as the courts are wont to hold from time to time, verbal consideration of my species of argument might dignify frivolity or lend it the color of merit. Naturally, silence is no deterrence to my likes, and in fact provokes me to produce interminable screeds and rants, wherein no doubt there is some merit worthy of judicious notice by the more patient and impartial arbitrator. Just as there is some truth in good humor, truth can be found as well in ill humor provoked by wounded pride. Of course all hell would break loose if everyone spoke their minds truthfully, for there is nothing as insulting as the god's truth about our selves; that is precisely why the gentry prefer to ignore it if not make jokes of it. The vulgar likes of me, raised in alleys where no holds are barred, would rather rake muck for amusement than hunt foxes or otherwise join like packs of peers in noble pursuits.

Notwithstanding its local virtues, The Miami Herald has its vices in common with other Establishment papers. They constitute a national propaganda organ for a single party, a party-paper we might as well call so-called Truth. Their differences are as superficial as the differences between the Democratic and Republican Parties. I mulled over Mr. Fielder's courteous rejection for two minutes. In the interest of striking a blow against America's version of Pravda, I hastily keyed the following Reply and clicked on Send before I had a chance to edit it:

DEAR TOM FIEDLER:

CORRECT ME IF I AM mistaken, but according your guidelines, it appears that the "credibility" you have identified depends on the gullibility of the public; i.e., the "market need", as assessed by those who have an interest in manipulating that market for personal and political gain.

As you know very well, many of today's "reputable" columnists cut their teeth not as reporters but as political hack writers; for instance, the right-wing ideologue Charles Krauthammer, whose reputation depends on his ability to perpetuate the divisive agenda of his fraction. And on the ideologically "liberal" side we have, for example, a "reputable" syndicated columnist with the New York Times, a divisive political-economist whose prejudice and downright personal hatred of so-called conservatives blinds him to any merits voiced on "the other side" as he is wont to define it.

As if there were only two sides to a solid issue. To take one of the sides, all a fool has to do is read up on the difference between conservative and liberal and how to be one or the other.

Neither side is “reputable” to the other; overall, both sides are disreputable to the public. In fact the newspapers are filled with political hack writers who "think in the box" and who perpetuate the continuous fragmentation of the moral (mental) integrity of their audience. The most irrational statements are made and passed off as reasonable to the unwitting. The like can be said of certain unnamed editors who write editorial opinions foolishly quoted by campaigning political candidates as oracles of truth: "Candidate Joe Blow's plan would sink every ship in the harbor." (The Miami Herald)

Today there exists a great "market need" for reasonable discourse that at least attempts to arrive at the truth of a subject from time to time no matter where that might land, instead of deliberately dividing the public and pandering to partisan prejudices which, when carefully examined, reveal how rotten the heart of corporate America has become.

The recent jingoistic conduct of the mainstream media in respect to the pre-emptive attack on the people of Iraq disgraced "this great nation of ours", and everyone of sound mind knows it. Although the rhetorical formalities were maintained, the differences between news, analysis, and opinion were substantially ignored,. In effect, news, analysis, and opinion, despite the formalities of style, amounted to advertising belligerent propaganda.

To justify the selling out of America by shifting the blame to the public is reprehensible in my opinion. The establishment's media does not really pander to the "market need" or the base credulity of the general public, but manipulates it while prostituting itself to the forces of darkness governing corporate board tribalism.

The Miami Herald needs a writer who thinks out of the box because he has never been in one. Don't you agree? That writer is me. Give me a call.

SINCERELY,
David Arthur Walters

ALTHOUGH I FOLLOWED up on many occasions, I never heard from Tom Fiedler again. Given the delusions of grandeur inherited from my father, I like to think that some of the provocations I sent to the Herald from time to time helped inspire the paper's muckraking department—its muckraking has been 'stellar' since the paper changed hands.

The Repetition Compulsion Of A Successful Loser

WHEN I AM ON THE VERGE of material success I am compelled to ruin my chances. I learned to control this virtually suicidal urge somewhat over the years. I succeeded in not ruining my opportunity until it was enormous and certain. And then unbearable anxiety would set in, and I would blow my top, blow everybody off.

Realizing that I had just done what I had sworn to never do again as long as I lived, I lived regretfully for some time thereafter.

And then I did it again: I made the worst career mistake in my life. Three months later an even greater opportunity arose because of that mistake, and then I blew that one. I was in a state of shock that I can only describe as utter panic. I had chosen penury over being somebody for millions of dollars.

The only thing I could salvage was my greed for knowledge in hopes of being wise one day, a foolish endeavor according to the Oriental sages. I retreated into the stacks of the library to be what I always wanted to be, and that was not an enormously powerful and wealthy person.

In fact, my phobia was the fear of owning property, of being burdened down with things, so I gave my last few things away and spent my life savings on my abstract pursuits. Of course my one and only goal was rather grandiose: Saving the world with me in it. My version of World Salvation included saving stuff people need and also stuff they want if that makes them happy and does not harm others.

My behavior was not unique. I have heard of the "fear of success" and the psychology thereof. I have tried some of the therapies to relieve myself of the condition. Sigmund Freud referred to the syndrome as repetition compulsion. He associated the habit with a so-called death instinct, and surmised that habit itself is a sort of petrifaction or deadness. I must add that habit is the biggest help we have.

Maybe my repetition compulsion was not suicidal after all. Could it be that I somehow did not want the material success at hand because I wanted some other kind of success, a success that seemed like failure to others?

Perhaps my two major failures, the biggest mistakes in my life, the ones that apparently ruined my chances of fame and fortune or at least considerable financial security in my maturity, were actually the best mistakes I had ever made in terms of being the so-called Nobody of the classics, the freelancer who lances the eye of the single-minded Cyclops so that he and his comrades can get away with the sheep.

Perhaps so-called failure was my success. I had stranded myself in an ark of civilization, a great library in the middle of nowhere. I was a complete failure, but I believed I was the richest man on Earth. I had no personal hope for success except to be one of the greatest authors the world would ever or never know, and I cared not which.

Well, now, having been taught by the works of the greatest authors I found in the stacks, I know I am not that great, but I stay on track, and I am happy with my small progress.

Ludwig Gumplowicz made me mad along the way because he said by the time one finds out what is really going on it is too late.

This all might seem to be "sour grapes" to those in want of other things, but the fruit is sweet to me. It is an escape from the pathetic little man that I was, into intercourse with the greatest minds, and for brief moments, the Mind.

My career is writing. I ask nothing for my work and expect nothing useful from it. I do appreciate everything I get, which over the last sixteen years is a few compliments, 16 Likes, and $50 from a Catholic magazine.

That's just how I am. I can't help it because I don't want to help it. I know people can understand how I feel, for we have some things in common.

Lately I have experienced some regret, almost enough to make a grumpy old man out of a happy-go-lucky fool. I need to get out and around, meet some people. Liz took me to Wal-Mart on the I-95. I got some badly needed shoes and two pairs of trousers. That adventure convinced me that I need to expand my horizons materially, find the means somehow to travel to those places in Europe I dreamed of visiting on a train. Maybe I can save the world with me in it after all.

Metamorphosis of a Bookworm

THE HAPHAZARD ARRANGEMENT of books and international collection of characters at Kafka's Kafé on Miami's famed South Beach is in fact absurd if not Kafkaesque.

For one thing, Timothy Leary would definitely love the decor. The visiting book browser or Internet surfer is greeted by a mural of a chocolate-colored butterfly-woman. A large caricature of Kafka painted on the ceiling looms above. Surreality is confirmed by an armless, surrealistically painted female mannequin, perchance dangled by the neck from the ceiling by misplaced machismo. The shelves are labeled, but more often than not the labels have little if any bearing on the books adjacent, and, even when properly shelved, each book is in constant danger of dislocation without notice to an unlikely shelf by shady-looking characters—it's the sunglasses—from every continent and island of the world.

Reticent intellectuals who find odd books of any note on the shelves but who do not want to purchase them, for a dollar (paperback) or three dollars (hardcover), tend to secrete them on the dusty tops of the bookcases, or else stuff them behind other books. Indeed, that is where I have found some of the better books, often mangy, dog-eared and brutally underlined. Before I learned all the ropes, I examined every shelf in the store, found a dozen books I liked and tucked them onto the end of a shelf by the crummy, Coke-stained old divan upstairs. Alas, they soon disappeared; some were purchased, others were hidden away by others for future reference. Indeed, I learned my lesson: Put the best books on top of the shelves, and stuff a few behind the outdated law books for good measure.

A hard-working, Argentinean American family man by the name of Oscar Deamici owns Kafka's, hence the place is often frequented by sundry familiars from Argentina. Internet access, computer sales and repairs is Mr. Deamici's main games. An Italian or two are sometimes around the place - many Argentinians are naturally frustrated Italians. Eccentrics drop by from time to time, including a twenty-something Mexican American, one of the great geniuses of the world. One of the few Wobblies still living drops by from time to time not to mention myself among several others who are inconspicuous in bizarre settings. By the way, a pleasant little café with sidewalk seating occupies the back of the store by the usually clean restroom - only one free-riding bookworm has been banned from Kafka's of late, not for his execrations but for his misplaced excretions.

The used books are literally thrown in for sake of the Other Revenue account. The book end of the business, with its inventory supported by fleeing residents and departing tourists, is the butt of Miami-Dade jokes; yet Kafka's is the best place in town to grab a trashy novel on the cheap, and, if a bookworm burrows long enough, he too shall have his reward. Of course the current newspapers in several languages and the glossy fashion and porno magazines are much in demand. Beware: one porno enthusiast, a respectable-looking Caucasian businessman, gets on the Internet from time to time, where he intently watches a video of a naked 300-pound woman bouncing up and down on something.

Despite the disheveled shelves, Kafka's clerks are intelligent, gregarious, and usually attractive. Cecilia from Argentina is one of Kafka's several Latina beauties. She is well versed in academic subjects, and her understanding and command of English is outstanding in case your Spanish is patetico. She is superstitious, at least to the extent of believing in diabolical possession after viewing the Emily Rose movie

- Emily purportedly sacrificed herself to prove the existence of God. Yet, on the other hand, Cecilia is an ardent intellectual *izquierdista* who enjoys Marx and Freud and is wont to deny the reality of every metaphysical notion including good and evil, notwithstanding her faith in the personifications of same - God and Satan – not to mention leftist ideology.

One evening while I was browsing books, Cecilia turned away from shelving books, and asked me, "What does nonfiction mean?"

"Why, uh, the label Nonfiction identifies all books that are not fiction," I begged the question.

She glanced confusedly at other labels on the shelves.

"Nonfiction is a general category," I continued. "Actually, the labels Biography, Science, Health, Sociology, History, Philosophy and so on belong to the category, Nonfiction. So the label, Nonfiction, if on the shelves, should be 'Other Nonfiction', meaning those books which are not fiction but are not otherwise classified. Sometimes we see the label, 'stories', which are connected narratives - they can be fiction or nonfiction."

"Hmm. So philosophy is not fiction?" she quizzed.

"No, philosophy is not fiction. Philosophy evolved from poetry and attempts to rationalize the intuition of truth. The ancient poets didn't make truths, they intuited truths and sang them - they composed or fashioned the poems that expressed or revealed truths. For example, the reasonable priests of Apollo at Delphi listened to the irrational cries of the pythia and rationalized them into rather bad verse."

"So philosophy is true?"

"Someone has said that philosophy is a lot of nonsense about common sense. Since common sense, when examined, can be absurd, philosophy rationalizes it. And philosophy is the search for wisdom, for understanding, getting to the bottom of what we know. Philosophers intend to express the truth, whatever that might be. Philosophy might express an ideal truth, and refer to ideas and ideals as reality. Therefore philosophy might not refer to tangible things and events, in the sense that they are capable of immediate sensory perception. But still we do not refer to philosophy as Fiction, because Fiction is our label for fictitious stories, novels, and.... Oh, you know what I mean."

"A novel is something new?" she asked, with eyes widening ever so innocently. She was pulling my leg and I fell over it. I continued with my abstruse pedantry since there seemed be an attentive ear for it.

"Cecilia, the adjective, 'novel', can mean something new or original, such as the news. When we use the word as a noun, 'novel' can indicate a novella, a short moral story, either true or false. But when speaking of books we generally use the word 'novel' to label long, imaginary stories about human beings, stories with plots. The stories in novels are fabrications or inventions of the mind. Of course novels might be filled with profound truths. Camus, a philosopher of The Absurd, said a good novelist must be a philosopher. So novels and other imaginary works are fiction, and the all rest is nonfiction. Don't you have that division in Argentina."

"Imaginary? Can't a novel be a true story about facts, a nonfiction story?"

"Yes, there's are historical novels, for instance this biographical novel, on the shelf here, about Michelangelo, *The Agony and the Ecstasy*."

"That's why it should be under 'Nonfiction'?"

"No, it should be under Fiction. In most American university libraries, we would find it under American Literature."

"But part of it is nonfiction," she affirmed.

"Most of it. The author, Irving Stone, is a great researcher, so his historical novels are like nonfiction histories, with some fictitious dialogue and fairly accurate descriptions of settings and people added. Come to think of it, Cecilia, I once thought I had discovered a largely ignored historical personage, someone whom I could write a book about, sell the movie rights, maybe make plenty of money."\"Really?"

Cecelia brightened up at the opportunity—despite her leftist leanings, she is bourgeois, and might take a shine to gold.

"Yes, I researched many histories, collected everything the historians said about my heroine. They had all copied one historian who was closest to the action, an American pioneer in popular history - it is amusing how a historian might get a Pulitzer Prize for what really amounts to plagiary, just putting a little spin on what others had written before him. Anyway, I was about ready to start writing the book, when it occurred to me that I should check the fiction catalog for mention of her name: Rachel Jackson, Andrew Jackson's wife. Not only had Irving Stone written a book about her, President's Lady, but a movie had also been made of the book. As for the historical novel, it amounted to some dialogue added to the material I already had in hand. There was very little fiction to the novel - it's just that the author had made a story out of the material."

"Oh."

"Yeah, that's what I said."

"Are nonfiction histories really true stories?"

"Good question, but come on, Cecilia, you're playing with me. I think you know the answer to these questions. The next thing you'll be asking is: What is the Truth? Histories might not be true but historians generally intend them to be true. Of course activist historians, knowing that history is necessarily limited by the historian's personal perspective, and knowing that history can really never be sufficiently accounted for or explained, use history to propagate their ideological agendas."

Cecilia, turning back to her task, looked at the title of a book, got on the step ladder and proceeded to shelve it. I admired her endowments - very Italian, lots of pasta and sauce, I thought. And I would have given a penny or two for her thoughts, for she often seemed lost in them. I certainly would not blame her for shelving books at random, I mused, for just plugging up the holes wherever they appeared. No matter where she put a particular book, it would wind up somewhere else, anyway, most likely under the wrong label, so why bother with categories in the first place? Heck, when customers ask if a certain kind of book is on hand, the insider is tempted to laugh out loud.

Left to myself again, I picked up the current copy of the Miami Herald from the rack. By chance, Rene Rodriquez' article plugging the new film, Capote, directed by Bennet Miller, caught my eye. Truman Capote had written what Ms. Rodriquez called an "indelible book", *In Cold Blood*, about the 1959 murder of the Clutter family by Perry Smith and Dick Hickock in Garden City, Kansas. I recalled that I had personally seen those killers in shackles, in the elevator at the courthouse in Topeka.

Capote, Ms. Rodriquez reported, is the first of two movies about the writing of *In Cold Blood*—another movie, Have You Heard? is scheduled for release in 2006. Truman Capote, she wrote, was 35 when he went out to Kansas to investigate the killings. Kansas! Oh, Gringo American that I am, how I miss Kansas and my old beer-drinking, pepper-eating Mexican friends!

"Six years later," she continues, "Capote instead wound up with a book that would invent a new publishing genre - the nonfiction novel - and would guarantee him his place in the canon of great American authors."

Nonfiction novel - a new publishing genre? Not true. The style is neither new nor novel. *In Cold Blood* is subtitled, A true account of a multiple murder and its consequences. That is what the work is: a true account, or, if you please, a true story, or a true mystery. It is not a novel. It is nonfiction: I looked it up the reference later and found it indexed in the Dewey Classification system as 364 - Criminology, and in the Library of Congress system as HV6533 – Criminology.

My considerations gave me cause to drift to the back of the store and pause at Kafka's little café, where I further considered the contemporary confusion of fiction with nonfiction. Now I have nothing against fiction on the whole: I prefer nonfiction; as for fiction, I want it steeped in truth. Reality has become so boring for some people that they must be constantly entertained; such is the enormity of the quantitative demand for instantly gratifying, superficial entertainment, only a supply of trash can meet it half way.

A recent example of the distaste for reality and a puerile affection for the shallow fancies of easily read trashy novellas came to mind over my café con leche at Kafka's. A certain critic who haunts the Web, Mister Netwit is his handle, was bored with one of my interview with a Cuban-American cubosurrealistic artist. The artist and I discussed our differing perspectives on Fidel Castro and the United States. During the interview, published almost verbatim, I advocated the free speech program I call 'Habla Libremente por Cuba', and argued that Mr. Castro's repression of dissent was foolish and contrary to the interests of the Cuban Revolution.

My free speech did not please Mister Netwit, and he felt free to say so. He said he had been to Cuba and was sick and tired of hearing the same old subjects aired. Of course mainstream media frequently airs those old subjects in South Florida because an intensely interested audience for them exists. But Mister Netwit was thoroughly bored. Nonetheless, he stooped to teach me how to write up an interview:

Turn it into a "story", a composition not altogether fictitious nor factual, but factious -an adjectival derivation from the nominal category he calls 'Faction.' Not a bad idea for someone who wants to entertain his audience with a novella; however, my intention was not to write a novella, but to transcribe a conversation for those who might or might not be interested in its content. Mister Netwit, however, believes that everything he reads should be, in the best of all possible worlds, 'Faction.'

At first glance I thought Mr. Netwit's 'Faction' was 'fiction' misspelled, for 'faction' refers to an abnormally contentious or self-seeking group within a larger group - a 'factious' party would be a contentious party. Perchance Mister Netwit and his ilk, to suit the confusion of reality with fantasy, unwittingly have a double-meaning in mind. "Use the fact to create fiction... faction," advised Mister Netwit.

After all, asked Mister Netwit, is not that why writers write? Do we not live to write Faction? That is, to tell fictitious stories, forgetting the other purposes of composition teachers tried to drum into our dense heads in high school.

Of course our teachers have been faulted for emphasizing exposition, which requires a great deal of hard thinking, over narration, description and persuasion. And now it appears that a certain faction of writers and teachers alike are wreaking vengeance on the honest person's penchant for nonfiction, abusing its facts by twisting them into a pack of lies, at worst, and half-truths, at best. The test of success: whether or not the resulting 'Faction' is an "easy read": Who wants to think hard nowadays, when we have a few experts and super-computers to do the grunt-work?

No doubt philosophers might say that Mister Netwit's faction corresponds with the fact that reality as we conceive it is an illusion. The truth is never wholly known, and what we know of it cannot be perfectly expressed no matter how concisely put in particular or general terms. Human expression is necessarily metaphorical and metaphysical; sentimental metaphor excites us more than arid metaphysics. Yet metaphysics, devoid of dirty details, is far more sublime. Certain Arab philosophers climbed their logical ladders to Supreme Being itself, and claimed from the summit that their transcendental mode was the higher way. Of course one might compose vulgar little stories to describe such being to those who are ignorant of it, and hence by indirection persuade them of the existence of ultimate reality.

Nevertheless, whether our subjects of interest are along the dirt road or at the end of the highway, honest writers will often draw a line, imaginary though it might be, between fiction and nonfiction, or rather between lies and truths, for truth is sometimes called fiction to protect the guilty. The faction that hews to faction has a right to their faction, and their intentional confusion of fiction with nonfiction might amuse us when we are out of sorts and do not want to know the difference between the two, but, in the final analysis or dissolution, the truth shall always preside over our cultivated domain. When the faction-writers know exactly what nonfiction is, we might turn to them for further advice.

I bade Cecelia adios and raced home high on caffeine, where I could not sleep nor focus on television's crime laboratories, not even the meat-puzzle of dismembered body parts. Staring at nothing as I lay on Elizabeth's borrowed air mattress, I mulled over my obsession with truth, whatever that might be, with wanting to know it and be it. My desire to tell only the truth and to be true to my self, whatever that is, came to me one cold day in Washington, shortly after I left the Nixon White House and stood in the center of the Library of Congress, imagining that I was absorbing all the knowledge therein. I was moved to examine my passport, and other identity documents in my wallet:

"That is not me!" I exclaimed, and threw the passport and wallet in the Potomac. "From here on out," I resolved, "I will be true to myself and speak only the truth." I'm afraid I have wavered since then, or rather careened off course! And here I am, on my back on an air mattress in South Beach, wondering why I am still so concerned with the difference between fiction and nonfiction.

What's the difference? The mind is plastic and is divided against itself in such a way that it can be self-employed to get us where we want to go. We aren't there now, so imagining that we are there as if we were there, as if our ideals are realized, is a fictional process and is writing fiction, is it not? I asked myself. And this kind of fiction can work, so it is useful fiction. So there is nothing wrong with the employment of useful fictions that help us realize the ambitions of our moral-social heritage. That does not mean we are liars.

Eureka! It came to me. The simplicity of it proved my gross ignorance all along, and caused me to remember how I was once angered by what a a Polish sociologist, jurist and political scientist by the name of Ludwig Gumplowicz said: By the time we find out what is really going on, it is too late to do anything about it.

Beneficial fictions appertain to the future, whereas lies appertain to the past and its culmination, the here and now. High hopes might be disappointed: live and learn, but keep Hope locked in Pandora's treasure casket for future motivation.

As everyone knows, lying can be harmful indeed. When we come to believe that fictions are true, it is then that our lies may cause us to unwittingly run amok and wreak havoc, as if we were paranoid little Hitlers with grandiose delusions. Take for instance the man who reads a book about the virtues of having a positive mental attitude and imagining and constantly affirming that he is God's gift to the world as if that were true in the here and now. What if he takes the suggestion to heart, and comes to believe that this fiction is actually true, and thinks that his mistakes, errors, faults, or sins are goods instead of evils?

I had almost drifted off to sleep when I heard a voice say something Ouspensky said long ago, that the change within will proceed when a man realizes that he does not have certain powers he ascribes to himself. Therefore, first of all, a man must not lie. He must know that he does not have something in order to make a genuine effort to get it. And he might have to pay dearly for what he thinks he already has.

God Playing Solitaire

THE SUBJECTIVE SELF OR SUBJECT STRIVES strives for knowledge of its unity in opposition to itself and splits into multiple representations to that end. The objective representations, however, cannot satisfy its impossible desire to know itself as a unity, for knowledge requires a minimum of two objects perceived by a subject; the subject without an objective body cannot be one of them; the consciousness of multiple representations would be divided among multiple representations and none of them would be the unity desired.

In fine, the subject cannot exist as a unity - its mission for self-knowledge as a unity is a mission impossible. The best it can do in its multiple representations is to imagine a coherent utopian state of absolute bliss in unity; but in fact such a state is static or lifeless - bliss is death. What the self really knows is change i.e. differences.

The phenomenal unity of self is the relation of contemplative self and active object in all perspectives; the possibility of self-knowledge, then, is not the knowledge of the unity of the self-in-itself, but rather the knowledge of the phenomenal relation of subject-object: two attitudes, through all windows.

In the futile struggle for knowledge of unity-in-itself, one might say that the multiplicity of the representative fragments of being strive to recover universal being, but cannot do so because of the particularity of their efforts to know themselves. It is as if fragments were shoved from universal being into individuality, and were condemned by the original sin of their birth to never recover their origin. The original sin is, of course, that of original being striving to know itself-in-itself; all fragments projected into space-time share that original sin, therefore must perish. Self-conscious humans have made a meaningful story of it:

"Why would we be subjected to suffering in this world unless we are being punished for a crime? Do not our fathers punish us for doing wrong? Must not eyes tally with eyes and teeth with teeth to balance the blood feuds? Justice must be done to right wrongs. Our race must have done something wrong, in the very beginning, to suffer these divisions. Therefore we have inherited our propensity to do evil to one another. Our suffering here at the hands of our father above is expiation for our original sin. We are born evil. Let us be loyal then, and in hate-based group-love find and expand our unity. To that end let us submit to our fathers, families, clans, nations, states, the universal world order, in the name of the first father."

Individual human beings suffer self-conscious life; they suffer consciousness of individuality. They are caught in a double-bind: they would recover original being or 'god', but that con-fusion would kill them as individuals, and would constitute, in effect, a particular suicide contrary to the will of the original project of universal being, to know itself through multiplicity. Hence the human imagines that his will is free while universal being arbitrarily and infinitely divides in contemplation of multiplicity. The particular self is not wholly free: although it retains a portion of the universal free will, it is confronted by the multiplicity of other individuals and the rest of the world. Hence the particular self imagines a free will not actually possessed. Its "free will" is partial, is an "illusion," albeit convenient for its toleration of the determined life.

The heroic aesthete, aware that his return as such to original being is impossible, contemplates his in-commutable, irreversible fate as a work of art or spectacular showing of fateful images. He recognizes and appreciates free will, unity of self, and other such notions - including even the notion of universal being contemplating itself through universally willed multiplicity - as entertaining illusions. It is not that he derives sado-masochistic pleasure from such entertainments. He genuinely appreciates the comedy of truth and tragedy of lie, as pastimes, as means by which time can be made tolerable and patience not over-taxed. He imagines Supreme Being playing games of solitaire.

The ethical individual naturally takes his life and his god very seriously. He is pressed all the while to decide between good and evil: Either/Or is his motto. That life is a play on the world-stage is of little comfort to the ethical individual. The spectacle does not compensate him for his anxiety and suffering: the part he plays torments him. He desperately wants the unity of supreme being and he denies the impossibility of having it.

Can we blame him? Some men would lose interest in life if they believed they were only actors (Gk. hypokrites) in scripted plays. Wherefore they imagine that they are captains of their souls and masters of their fates, believe that they can master and change the very form of their soul and world, if not this world, then the next. They even imagine this mastery while denying it, projecting their will onto Supreme Being and imagining themselves as slaves. In their arrogance they profess humility, oblivious to their own hypocrisy. They learn to believe in their illusions as a matter of subconscious habit. They are confident, they are with faith, they have blind faith; otherwise the facts would cause them to despair. As for the facts confronting faith, they are vanities; the complexities perceived are illusory and ephemeral: only being or god is permanent. How being differs from nothing is unknown.

If we are to follow the reasoning at the top of this page, the ethical humans are quite right! But the heroic aesthete calls the ethical men and women unheroic fools for really believing in the ultimate vanity, the Vanity of vanities, and the illusory myths attached thereto. Maya, said the yogi, is a synonym for ignorance. The aesthete sometimes envies ignorant fools.

At least the illusion of free will behind Either/Or behind the feeling of merit and demerit, praise and blame, innocence and guilt reinforces the feeling of unity, and, at the same time, the psychology of violence and disorder in human life as particular lives struggle for individual life and, at the same time, death in universal being through hate-based group-love and the like projects.

Working against its unity in multiplicity, continuation of the illusory spectacle is assured no matter how brutal and cruel, so that men do not despair and do what an insane man would do if he really wanted the wholeness of sanity or immediate unity with the all - destroy himself. But alas, that would leave all behind, so life goes on.

ANTONIA, A POEM IN Memory of Anthony Lewis

SURELY NOTHING MORE pure than thee
Slumbers in Mother Night's embrace;
Surely to-night no fuller Moon
Resembles well thy sweet pale face,
Framed by locks fair and confidence
Of your faithful midnight prayer.

YET, IN A CAVE BY JEALOUS Moon,
Reside three Fates dressed all in white,
All of them daughters of black Night:
Clotho the Spinner loves to spin;
Lachesis draws what has been spun;
Atropos severs life's frail thread
Suspended between gloom and gloom.

WHOSE BECK AND CALL Fates might answer
Is often hotly contended;
But rest assured, Antonia,
While in your precious innocence
Rest may so easily obtain.
For, restless in his bestained bed,
Ambrosio twists and turns with
Lust and guilt against his poor vows.

AMBROSIO, AMBROSIO,
Whom conscience has torn asunder.
Lies concealed in his monkish cell;
But not from mannish Matilda,
Demonessa, urging him on,
Nor from his holy Deity,
Counseling virtuous restraint.
Hence Aye and Nay dance in tandem
Until vile incestuous rape
And foul murders are committed
And duly punished by Devil
Doing God's will as commissioned.

THEN, ONLY THEN SHALT thou molder
As thy mother Elvira molds
Whilst Ambrosio, cast into
The chasm of hopeless despair,
Impaled upon the hellish rocks
So far below the gaze of God,

Slowly fulfills his Agony.

MATTHEW LEWIS (9 JULY 1775 - 10 May 1818) was a peculiar fellow. His behavior today might cause him to be identified as a goth.

Like Mary Shelley, Lewis made an enormous impact with his only novel, The Monk, which more-or-less defined the far edge of sensational Gothicism when it was published in 1796. He went on to write a number of plays, poems, and translations, many of which featured Gothic themes and motifs.

As a playwright Lewis was rather successful, his melodramatic flair finding an appreciate audience in the days of Romantic drama. Lewis abandoned the theater when he inherited his family's West Indian sugar plantations

Maya is Real

MAYA IS A MIGHTY TOUCHY SUBJECT, difficult if not impossible to comprehend. "By his powers of maya, Indra goes around in many forms." Alas, the heroic warrior-god Indra was not the only god with mayic powers. He supplanted the magnificent *mayin*, Varuna, god of justice and order, the guardian of fertile waters who had stood in the firmament and used his mayic power to measure out the earth, as it were, with a measuring stick - estimated to be about a yard long. And Indra himself would eventually be demoted to a relatively minor status within the pantheon.

The term 'maya' is derived from 'ma', meaning, to measure out, that which measures out and limits. Hence maya is the power of measurement. Man refers to his own *mayic* power with the term 'manu' or 'man', meaning, he who measures out thought - a mother or mama measures out creation - her children. As Protagoras said, Man is the measure of all things, those that are, that they are, those that are not, that they are not; but Protagoras did not mean that subjective individuals are *mayins* or that man is the creator of the objective universe. The meaning of abstract maya is threefold: in maya we have a trinity: creative power, creating, creation. That is, the Maker, Making, Made. Or, Cause, Force, Effect.

Now we recall that some time after Varuna measured out the creation, Vrita the river-dragon had a considerable power of his own, the power of envelopment. Vrita seized the fertile rivers from their guardian Varuna and holed up with the treasure in his ninety-nine fortresses. Indra—properly known as the truth that makes the knowers of it immune from punishment no matter what they do—got drunk on soma and slew Vrita with a thunderbolt. Wherefore the just and sometimes merciful Varuna was demoted because he had failed to personally keep the rivers within their beds. Varuna—a white man in golden armor seen riding a sea-monster and carrying snake-lasso—would henceforth be a sort of watchman over the rivers and oceans, while Indra lorded it over the creation. Indra would eventually have to make way for Visnu and Siva—Indra was demoted to preside over lesser gods and over the weather.

Individual men have reason to believe that they own maya and are therefore able to craft creation as they wish. On second thought, we have sufficient cause to believe that maya is not possessed by men but that men are possessed by maya. Indeed, Maya's fools are infinite in number. Even wise men have died in vain attempts to define maya. Just last week, two sages were mortally wounded when their dispute over maya's true nature came to blows. They had agreed, first of all, that maya was god's power, and that it was indescribable. But then they tried to describe it, and got into a heated argument over whether or not maya can be terminated by right knowledge; whether or not it has a beginning; whether or not it both projects and veils the universe; whether or not it is the nature of existence; whether it is in the individual or the absolute or in both. And finally, they disagreed on their premise, that maya is indescribable, and went after each other with scissors.

Since all men and women are born of woman, woman originally gets the blame for such madness. The original mayas were gnas, the celestial wives of the gods. Abstractly speaking, gna is the feminine principle, a principle that is, according to the testimony of many men, far more deceptive than the male principle. Maya was first of all the cosmic mother and the world-goddess. Aristocratic mayas were the consorts of male gods. The ordinary maya is a temptress or feared woman. A woman who really knows her maya turn a warrior into a pussycat and have him eating out of her hand. In the Mahabharata, the god uses his maya to delude mankind, to play with people as if they were toys. Of course women alone not to mention Venus are not really to blame for maya, the illusory, beguiling power, although their natural difference gives them cause to master it. Men of course have a hand in their own illusions and delusions - they are self-deluded to some extent. The erotic power makes two tangle. We are better off blaming our own ignorance than maya. Incidentally, according to some schools of thought, maya is a synonym for ignorance (*ajnana* and *nescience* or *avidya*).

Perhaps it is ignorance that leads men to believe that ignorance is caused by a certain and deliberate power, a divine power with two faculties: to project the world (*viksepa*), and cover or hide the truth (*avarana*). Some fakirs claim that this world is the one-god's sport or play because god has a whim to be many instead of one; those of us who are many are bewildered as a consequence of the projected divisions of the one; the truth is hidden by a cosmic veil; only a few fakirs can pierce that veil and be liberated from this illusory grinding up of the one - we can thank god that they might choose to stay behind and lead the rest of us out of our confusion. If only we really understood that the apparent multiplicity of our world is 'maya'—our ignorance and illusion—the unreality negating the one true reality—we could cast off nature-ignorance, the mass delusion of the space-time continuum, and reside in blissful truth. How that bliss differs from death or nothingness is subject to further speculation.

With the advent of modern science, the term 'maya' is most often employed in reference to feats of magic and illusionism. That is not to say that the prehistoric superstition attributing changes to the magical power of deities instead of natural forces has been extinguished in the popular mind. A secret *mayic* cult in Manhattan limits admission to applicants who can jump through a plate glass door without breaking the glass.

Sri Tundraputa claims they are wasting plate glass, for anyone possessed of the yogic powers can, for example, transform themselves into a subatomic particle, race though the earth and come out the other side with the greatest of ease. The plate glass is an illusion, he says, but it is a real illusion, and should not be bother with as such. He pointed out that although the oldest scripture in the world, the *Rgveda*, sings of the power of deities to change shape and create illusory effects, nowhere do the Vedas question the reality of the illusory forms, no matter how incomprehensible those forms seemed at the time.

"Maya is the real cause of the material world," insisted Tundraputa. "Maya is just another name for Siva's guided energy, Sakti, or the *mula-prakriti* evolving as the phenomenal universe. Existence is necessarily restrained by maya. Time restrains eternity, hence we have mortality. Space restrains omnipresence, thus we have individuality. Desire restrains perfection, consequently we have incessant activity and suffering. Learning limits omniscience, therefore our ignorance. Dependence limits omnipotence, fatality is the result. Our relation to the Lord is restrained by limitations obscuring the Lord. The Lord's creation is especially obscure for those Westerners whose knowledge is limited by subject-predicate linguistics and the logical subject-object or experiencer-experienced static dichotomy. Jumping through plate glass windows might get disillusioned kids into hospitals and mental wards, but they will soon be disillusioned with disillusionment or enslaved by insanity, an unwholesome liberation."

If I Were A Christian

ALTHOUGH I AM NOT A CHRISTIAN, I have been unavoidably influenced by Christianity: I have lived my entire life in the Judaeo-Christian culture. Of course I have had many encounters with other faiths and cultures, seemingly exotic to me because of my own cultural conditioning, which certainly made the exotic appealing. During my youth, many of my comrades were mouthing phrases such as God is Money, or God is Society, or God is Nothing, and what not. Most popular of all was God is Dead, and that was Good News to juvenile delinquents: it signified the Gospel of Rebellion rather than the bad news of parental authority.

When it dawned on me that God might not have existed in the first place, I eagerly devoured all the atheistic tracts I could get my grubby hands on. My favorite atheists were the most intelligent ones, those educated by Christians: the Jesuit schools produced some of the best atheists, some who returned as guest speakers on the existentialist circuit.

In retrospect, I really did not learn anything from the Christian atheists that I could not have discovered from the Christian faithful first hand. As my dance master Luigi said when he heard I was taking lessons from one of his students: "Why are you going there when God is here?"

Nevertheless, because of several sorry experiences with professed Christians, I eventually avoided all contact with them all. Just the mention of Jesus the Christ was enough for me to break off a relationship. As far as I was concerned at the time, the word 'Christian' was a synonym for 'hypocrite.' I could have cared less about Jesus, who seemed to be an adult version of the child's Imaginary Friend, and I was convinced that the expression Jesus Loves You must be one of the biggest lies Man has ever told to itself.

But my heart was changed by life's several lessons. For instance, I learned that hypocrisy, including my own, is not a property peculiar to Christians, but is rather the crisis underlying the entire human race. Furthermore, given the spiritual poverty of human relations, some real person if not Jesus, had better love everyone. For Christians, that person is naturally Jesus, and by His example I hope that someday all Christians can truly love one another and non-Christians like me just as well, instead of using Jesus Loves You as a substitute for the love they lack.

Therefore, I often find myself rooting for Christians. And even more so since I realized that my complaints against them were actually due to disappointment with certain "Christian" ideas implanted in me, ideas nearly impossible to uproot. Nonetheless, because of other personal predilections, I do not expect to be "saved" by Jesus in this life, nor do I anticipate professing any organized faith whatsoever. However, considering the professed need for the appearance of Jesus Christ on Earth, I want to make a few crude remarks as an unfaithful outsider about what I see as a serious threat to Christian faith in the existence of Christ - I mean actual, down-to-Earth existence, not the nebulous ideality people miscall reality because they want it to be real since they cannot stand the reality given to them.

It is no accident that I raise the crucial question as Christmas approaches: it is the critical question at the very crux of Christianity. It has been argued so many times that the real significance of Jesus the Christ has become generally neglected. Instead, whether Santa Clause exists or not is the central topic of Christmas, making the Advent, the suffering of labor and the joy of birth, a mere occasion for childish amusement. It is not that the question has been made moot by the living FACT. No, as a matter of fact, it seems that many Christians grew so weary of the real battle that they left the matter to be tried by experts, with the result that Jesus Christ, Man-God, has been almost entirely replaced by words signifying nothing except the caviling of those who use their intellect to avoid the living, working FACT.

In fact, the mere logic of god called "theology" became, for lack of faith in the FACT, a big cover up, a history of lies about God and therefore a subtle indictment of the personal Supreme Being. Jesus the Christ, God incarnate, is stolen and carefully hidden away in a metaphysical closet where nobody can see "Him"; thus is the Father and the motherly Holy Spirit rendered invisible as well. Eventually the Sword of Jesus was taken from the sheath and handed to the political authority to forestall the violent revolution required for the realization of the Kingdom of God on Earth; the prince in turn guarantees the safety of the theological caste, and conducts his wars in the name of God for alleged defense of the Faith. Thus it is impossible to know whether the professors of faith are atheists or theists; given their logical absurdities and the discrepancy between faith and works, the word "Nothing" could be substituted for "God" and one would be unable to ascertain the difference of meaning if any between the two terms.

Just as theology has served in practice to defame God, secular history, written as a woeful litany of man's crimes against himself, is a self-indictment. Church and State are partners albeit each might deny or ignore the other in name: Religion worships Power while Politics distributes it. Instead of exposing Man's essential goodness, which is the real cure for his illness, a fortune is made by dogmatically denouncing him and persuading him that there can be no Heaven on Earth or Christ walking on it let alone on water. Of course, if man will only make the necessary sacrifices, pay the requisite fees and deference to received authority, be defined and controlled according to false science, then his good fortune is guaranteed in the next life or at least he will lead a pleasant life in the present world, have sufficient social security, perhaps strike it rich or just be your average blessed bloke.

By nature we imitate and emulate to survive. We tend to go along with our secular and spiritual authorities because we rightfully fear anarchy. Yet we have gradually lost confidence in hierarchical authority itself. If there is a cunning Spirit of History it is the Spirit of Freedom. Now that we approach freedom from everything including personal authority, we face the chaos of diffidence, non-differential and -deferential Equality; to wit, Nothing. There is a pervasive fear that the situation is hopeless both here and in the Beyond; if there be a Beyond: that is why Having Faith requires such a desperate struggle as the herd disintegrates.

True faith requires no arguments and its public virtue is self-evident in witnessing. But what medicine do the spiritual doctors both secular and religious give us? Words and words and more words about abstract utopias, paradises, promised lands, and other nowheres invariably bearing the very logical defects of the desperate conditions they are abstracted from. But Christianity gives us the living FACT of Jesus the Christ, does it not? Jesus is not merely an arbitrary name of a concept, but the Name of the Real Man who is God Himself! Is that not so?

Not according to many Christian experts who follow in the footsteps of the thinkers who stole Jesus the Christ from believers and hid him away somewhere, God only knows where. Forget the scriptures, they say, and resort to allegorical interpretations, to mythological musings, to hermeneutics, the Science of Interpretation invoking Hermes, son of Zeus and Maia, the god of trickery and cunning, a thief who became messenger of the pagan gods - yes, I know, the Egyptian Hermes Trismegistus is meant, but still Thoth was corrupted by the Greeks. Therefore the only way for anyone to find the stolen Jesus or to know the unknown God is to enroll at the temple and become privy to the esoteric teachings of the hermeneutic authorities.

Once one has access to the higher knowledge merely symbolized by the scriptures, he will know more about God than even highly educated people, never mind the ignorant sheep whom he is certified to counsel regarding ultimate matters - matters that must remain arcane for their own good. Hence between the flock and their shepherds is an ugly hypocritical chasm.

As for the mundane Jesus, the Historical Jesus, modern scholars have deemed Him irrelevant to the present circumstances; in any event, if He did exist, historical knowledge of Him can be disposed of as unnecessary to the faith in words instead of works.

You see, what is important is whatever we might feel and believe now; and we are to feel and believe what the authorities, who are in-the-know, see fit to preach. In other words, Jesus does not exist except as he is preached: we have not a Historical Jesus, but a Preached Jesus. Or some prefer a Mythical Jesus evolving pursuant to the Gospel of Reason; Jesus then is the result of a constant argument, rather than the living FACT that He is, was and always will be.

If I were a Christian, I would not take the FACT out of the heavenly light and replace it with abstract rationalizations. Come to think of it, how absurd it is that many Enlightenment thinkers, with their faith in Reason to expose the progressive revelations of God, reduced Jesus and God to their own idea or thoughts based on no FACT, while out of the other side of their mouths they spoke of scientific evidence!

Moreover, thinking of thinking, I think my faith would certainly be on shaky grounds if I were to believe Jesus is just an idea or a concept to be continuously rationalized, or something emitted from God, just a phantasm, a sort to White Lie told by God. And how could I still have faith and believe that, even if the Historical Jesus did exist, the Historical Jesus does not matter, or that he was "just a man"? May Zeus forbid! for that could only be true if Jesus the Christ is a Stranger and God an Alien.

Yes, I do realize that facts often tend to stand in the way of religions rather than support them: even though I belong to no religion, I have often said, "To Hell with the facts!" Facts can be most contemptible indeed, especially when they obstruct us, but many thinkers learned to cherish them. The old sensist philosophers demanded sensory evidence as proof for their arguments, and soon argued God right out of existence or made God into a fantasy or an empty shell of an idea better called Nothing and kept secret if still believed in lest the devotee be laughed at or scorned for a truly nondenominational religion—Nothing is indivisible.

Indeed, one can have faith in Nothing, but he shall always be suspected of atheism. I am not one to condemn faith in the Invisible per se, but I believe, when the Invisible is taken to the extreme, it denies the very basis of Christianity: that God is a living Fact as the Son right here on Earth for all to see and bear witness to. In fact, if I were a Christian, I would demand to know Jesus the Christ as the Evidence and Proof of God.

But I am not a Christian. I enjoy the privileges of all heresies and of atheism. I am free to think that Jesus the Christ is the Perfect Sign of God as Man; the actual Reconciliation of Body and Spirit; the Most Excellent Synthesis of Thesis and Antithesis; the Perfect I AM; the actual living presence as Love in accord with Law; the Eternal Gospel embodied and much more, including the Harmony of every contradiction you might think of. But what do I know? Nothing.

Because of the influence of Christians and because of my sympathy for those who suffer the human predicament, it pains me to see professed Christians deny by their deeds if not by their theological words the living FACT presented, especially during their own holidays, such as Christmas. Santa might be fun, but whether Santa exists or not is of small consequence to me except for the pleasure of seeing children smile; I expect no presents from Santa nor do I deserve any. Christmas itself, as far as I am hopeful, might constitute the ultimate presentation of Man's greatest gift.

There are still many in the modern world who truly love the real Jesus the Christ. I will not join their church, but I am happy for them as long as they do not try to save me.

The Little Hitler in Everyone

AN INDIVIDUAL WOULD PERSIST FOREVER and ever if it could, brooking no opposition to its persistence. Nonetheless, lacking resistance the anarchistic individual would not even exist as such, would not be in-dividual or divided into megalomaniacal subject and resisting object. That is, the irrational root of violence is within and is the individual factor of the personal equation - a person is the free-willing individual socially conditioned.

Infants are natural-born revolutionaries. They feel omnipotent at first, and tend to revolt against restraints until they learn that total resistance is futile if not downright dangerous. Yet the omnipotent feeling persists throughout the social development of the individual, and, to one extent or another, the resulting person lives under a certain delusion of grandeur, believing at least secretly that the world is at his beck and call, that he is at least in part its savior. Of course the all-important person's delusion is one of persecution when he feels that the whole world is against him.

An "insane" or unwholesome delusion of grandeur may in certain "heroic" cases take on a "sane" or wholesome appearance, and become a popular illusion. A mirage of an oasis or a hero appears to thirsty or power-hungry travelers. A crowd of individuals, lacking the power of leadership, project their own native feeling of omnipotence or freedom onto an individual, recognizing him as a "great man" or "hero," the very man who can quench their thirst for power. Enamored by the illusion of absolute freedom, they eagerly forsake what remains of their own freedom, and their idol absorbs every drop.

Adolf Hitler, to take an egregious example, was sincerely perceived by the great majority of Germans as their Teutonic messiah. His ascent to power was quite easy, for he was building a shadowy state of disgruntled authoritarians within the purportedly democratic state all along.

Now every school child knows about the Beer Hall Putsch, how Hitler got off easy with a short prison sentence, a great opportunity to write about his revolutionary struggle. And we all know about the Red Scare the Nazis provoked with the February 27, 1933 Reichstag Fire. And of course the threat of Bolshevist terrorism among other emergencies called for the March 23, 1933 Enabling Act - the "Law for Removing the Distress of People and Reich" - which gave legislative power to the Reich cabinet and legalized in advance decrees that "might deviate from the Constitution." We remember well the July 14, 1933 decree making the Nazi party the only lawful party in the Fatherland:

"The National Socialist German Worker's Part constitutes the only political party in Germany. Whoever undertakes to maintain the organizational structure of another political party or to form a new political party will be punished with penal servitude up to three years or with imprisonment of from six months to three years, if the deed is no subject to a greater penalty according to other regulations."

Many of Hitler's storm troopers were disaffected workers who expected him to fulfill his promise of a social revolution and to militarize the SA. No way. There would be social revolution or any other revolution for that matter, not after Hitler's political revolution. For Heaven's sake, Hitler needed industrialists and big businessmen. Unions had to be dissolved and workers virtually indentured to realize their true virtue - they were glad to have jobs and cheap recreation to boot. In fact, Hitler clearly stated on July 6, 1933, that revolution would not become a permanent state of affairs, that "good businessmen" were quite welcome under his regime even if they were not Nazis - and business prospered despite the enormous bureaucracy set up to rationalize his political economy and to collect bribes.

After President Hindenburg died on August 2, 1934, Hitler combined the offices of president and chancellor in himself, becoming the Fuehrer and Reich Chancellor. On August 19, 1934, 95 percent of registered voters approved of Hitler's seizure of absolute power. Did he in fact take the following oath to himself?

"I (Adolf Hitler) swear by God this sacred oath, that I will render unconditional obedience to Adolf Hitler, the Fuehrer of the German Reich and people, Supreme Commander of the Armed Forces, and will be ready as a brave soldier to risk my life at any time for this oath."

A survivor of Hitler's egomaniacal reign of terror claimed that a little hitler exists in everybody.

The Devil Was In The Snot

THE MAJOR GOAL OF ENTHUSIASM in the public and private sectors today is growth in production and consumption. The progress has been phenomenal since the industrial revolution. An alien from a spiritually inclined planet would think humans had been fatally possessed by demons after observing our race to produce and consume ever more and our frantic effort to pave over most of the world while cluttering up the rest.

That is, "enthusiasm" is definitely restricted to interests leading to the purchase and possession of mass-produced goods and services. Many people are possessed by their possessions, as if some sorts of spirits resided therein. Yet the power elite denounce those who oppose such demonically inspired gross materialism as the bedeviled and accursed "forces of darkness," or as mentally ill and in dire need of serotonin reuptake inhibition.

Spirituals disagree with the secular authority's definition because genuine enthusiasm is about God and nothing less. After all, enthusiasm means "god-possessed," and not greed-possessed or lust-possessed.

Anyone uneasy with the hyperactive and demented society of consumption may seek solace in one church or the other, hopefully to be possessed by peace if not by the Holy Spirit. Yet that retreat is no sanctuary to the lone wolf who knows that modern churches are contaminated and possessed by the apotheoses of the social disease in question. Wolves are, like humans, hierarchically organized, but they too have their anarchists, the lone wolves. The lone wolf knows his god can only be found in Natural Religion, in a forest under a banyan tree, or perhaps in a desert cave, or at least in an unregulated monastery.

Organized religion does not provide the viable alternative that the lone wolf, who seeks peace in the "solitary death," unconsciously craves. He knows his freedom is not in a monastery where obedience to church authority is the divine rule. No, he longs for the cave from which he descended eons ago to herd and farm and to found towns. But the town no longer wants the wolf who founded it, except in an iron cage. The church would also cast him out as a heretic, or keep him locked in a dungeon to be periodically tortured by the Iron Maiden.

The lone wolves, who originally founded religions and now threaten them, are for the most part ascetics who forswear production and consumption in order to obtain union (yoga) with their god. They might not make a go of it entirely alone: they might gather together in secluded retreats. Independent individuals and groups were perceived by the Roman Church as a serious threat to its authority, for yoga or direct communion with the deity, enthusiasm or god-possession, takes the individual out the centralized Church's sphere of authority.

Decentralization, tolerance, plurality of views, religious freedom can be detected in India under the Hindu umbrella religion, but not in the Roman Church. The Church, as it gained power, did everything in its power to bring enthusiasm to heel, to bring monks together in monasteries to support and obey the dictates of the Roman authorities. It encountered many difficulties along the way with heretics, people who had the audacity to "choose" for themselves.

One such curious group of heretics was the Messalians, a sect that supposedly originated in Mesopotamia about 360 A.D. "Messalians" is Syrian for "those who pray." Our knowledge of their doctrines and practices is derived solely from the discriminatory denunciations of the authorities, wherefore we may examine the behavior of the Messalians in that reflected light, as presented in the works on heresy penned by Theodore, Timothy Constantinople, and John of Damascus:

Prayer is the only way to salvation. Zealous prayer drives out the indwelling demon each person was born with (including the Apostles) ever since the first parent Adam. Only prayer can root out the indwelling Satan that urges the person do evil.

Messalians jump over demons cast out of their runny noses, or in spit, or sometimes in the forms of fire, smoke or serpents. They shoot at the demons with their fingers as if their fingers were arrows. Constant praying keeps the Messalians from talking as wildly as they are wont to do. When the praying casts out the demon, they achieve Apathetic (apathy), the reception of the Holy Spirit, which is a marriage to the Bridegroom of Heaven, just as a woman receives a man.

Once a Messalian has achieved Apatheia, which he feels and perceives as the Holy Spirit dwelling within, his body is freed from passion and his soul is set free: he needs no further restraint or teaching. Any wantonness or licentiousness thereafter is not sinful because it is done without passion.

The Messalians see things to come. The actually see the invisible Trinity as One. They see the Cross of Light. They foretell the future and engage in fortune-telling frauds.

Manual labor and giving to the needy are anathema to Messalians, for Messalians are the "poor in spirit," the truly "spiritual" beings. They sleep most of the day, pretending to be in prayer. They sleep to dream, dream to prophecy, and, being deceived, prophecy to deceive.

They do go along with the sacraments from time to time, perhaps to fit in without hypocrisy to their faith, for they believe such things do no harm or good.

John of Damascus said, "Among them they have contempt for the churches and their altars, as it were fitting for ecclesiastical ascetics not to attend synaxes and yet hold prayers in their oratories: for they say that such is the power of their praying that the Holy Spirit appears perceptually to them and those instructed by them....Those who come to them without any fruit of repentance from various sins, without authority of priests, without the stages which are prescribed in the ecclesiastical canons, they promise to take away every sin immediately, only if someone undertakes the prayer which is much spoken among them, and thoughtlessly becomes an initiate of their trickery." (*De Haeresibus*)

References in sacred literature were made to the Messalians of Mesopotamia in the 370s, in Asia Minor in the 420s and 430s, and the Council of Ephesus condemned them in 431. Writings about them circulated widely thereafter, playing a key role in the Byzantine monastic revival of the 8th and 9th centuries, and in the Hesychast movement of the 14th century.

The actual identity of the Messalians is controversial. The designation was applied to anyone who was unenthusiastic about manual labor and sacrificial ordinances, anyone who placed emphasis on the experiential, emotional aspects of religion and who believed prayer could make the soul divine and immortal. They reportedly wandered from place to place, slept in the streets, and took up no occupations except their fervent prayer.

So-called Messalians were persecuted. For instance, Letoius, Bishop of Militene, burned monasteries where this form of Quietism was found, "driving the wolves from the sheepfold." Many suspected Messalians were put to death by the Christian magistrates.

As enthusiastic as we may be about the freedom of our individual spirits, let us bring this ancient example of enthusiasm to a close with a silent prayer for the Messalians In the Name of the Past, the Present, and the Future, as One.

REFERENCES:

THE CATHOLIC ENCYCLOPEDIA, New York: Encyclopedia Press 1911

Columba Stewart, *Working the Earth of The Heart, The Messalian Controversy in History, Texts, and Language to AD 431*, Oxford: Clarendon: 1991

Ghoul News

GHOULS NEWS KNOWS WHAT WE ARE AFRAID OF—crime and unruly nature—so it daily dishes out hours and hours of crime and weather news. Syria sometimes seems to be a more civil and pleasant place to live, at least in terms of total body count and icy roads.

Ghoul News goes over and over the same crimes so that everyone tuning in will know about the baby found in a bag, the single and double- and triple-murders, how many toughs raped the teenager and for how many hours, so on and so forth, the usual gruesome fare that gets high ratings. Yet one wonders if the violent refrain really serves the purposes of repetition, say, of cautioning people: after all is done and said, the crime rate does not go down despite the lurid sensationalism.

A steady diet of local news might turn a man into a ghoul. He will know something is wrong when the sight of the heterosexually paired announcers, the Muppet-looking info-babes, start making him sick by association with news content, and he begins to wish that the broadcasting network would regularly rotate them out of sight, bringing in fresh faces, perhaps a few ugly people with grim countenances to match the local news. Of course there is no such thing as an "ugly" human being, but I think you know what I mean.

Ironically, at the time violence coverage was increasing on the networks, the crime rate was actually going down. Go figure why....

Also by David Arthur Walters

The Seed That Fell On Rocky Ground
South Beach Florida Coronavirus Panic 2020
The Yellow Vest Movement
Signs of Madness
The Compassionate Heart of America
My Hawaii Nei
The Amazing South Beach HDD Sewer Project
Tracey's Secret
The Amazing Kansas City Library
The Helgalian Chronicles
The Espanola Way of Doing Business
Katherine Sergava
No Hard Feelings - A Dancer's Reflections
Sovereign Immunity - The Debasement of the United States
Helene and Paul - A Characterological Romance
Anarkhia
Random Ramblings
Melange
Ideology aka Idiotology
Accounts Payable - My Life Past Due
The Sly Way Gurdjieff & Ouspensky
Groundhog Days - Timely Intercourse
The Black VIrgin
APXH - Wicked Political Musings
Open Publishing

My Hand

www.ingramcontent.com/pod-product-compliance
Lightning Source LLC
LaVergne TN
LVHW050552160826
845677LV00011B/2281